Warning Signs

Dr. Gist —
Keep doing what you do — you're touching many lives!

Danielle
Feb. 2013

Warning Signs

What every woman should know
A dating guide

DANIELLE E. WARD

AMBERGRIS PRESS

Copyright © 2013 by Danielle E. Ward
First Edition

Ambergris Press
P.O. Box 7364
Flint MI 48507-0634
1.810.444.4513
www.ambergrispress.com

All rights reserved. No part of this book may be reproduced in any form or transmitted in any form or by any electronic or mechanical means including information storage and retrieval systems without prior written permission from the publisher, except for the inclusion of brief quotations in a review.

Publisher's Note: Names and identities have been changed to protect confidentiality. Any similarity to people living or dead is purely coincidental.

Library of Congress Control Number: 2012922303
ISBN: 9780988624696

Printed and bound in the United States of America

Dedication

To women who are ready
to move toward healthy relationships

Acknowledgements

I thank God for the ideas that flowed every time I sat down to write. This book would not have been completed without His guidance.

Jamila, you helped me lay the groundwork for the book. Finally, a finished product!

Elijah, I am so glad to have you as my son! I am grateful for your ability to self-entertain while I was writing, and for sharing your opinion whenever I asked. It may have seemed like I would never finish, but I did and now you can have me back, 100%.

Mom and Dad, you have been some of my biggest cheerleaders anytime I endeavored to try something new. Thank you for your feedback and unwavering support while I completed this book.

Brenda, you were the first to read through the entire manuscript. I appreciate your insightful input. Thanks also for your sage counsel regarding my self-care throughout the entire process.

Eric and Joyce, thank you for your recommendations on what to include in the book. The book would not have been complete without them.

Shaun, you've been an integral part of the whole process. You listened to me when I was excited, overwhelmed, frustrated and eager, but unsure of what to do next. Thank you for being a sounding board and offering your advice.

Duane, you helped me transform my cover from an idea in my head into a tangible product. I am truly thankful for the time you dedicated to me while in the midst of your own projects.

Gary, your eagle eye is valued more than words can express. Thank you for your attention to detail and clear, concise critiques of my manuscript. You helped me step up my game.

Jacinta and Ken (Image Graphics & Design), it was such a pleasure to work with you during the typesetting phase of the book. Your professionalism and friendliness made the experience a pleasant one.

Shana (Arbor Indexing), job well done on the indexing. That was a mountain I was more than willing to let someone else climb!

Jan, David, Courtney and Marcellus, I thank you for being willing to help a fellow author. The time and experiences you shared helped me immensely, especially during those times when I felt lost in the details.

Those of you who always asked me, "How's your book coming along?" kept me motivated to continue plodding ahead so I'd have something new to report. Thank you for keeping me on my toes.

This has definitely been a learning adventure and I am thankful to everyone who encouraged me during my journey.

Danielle

Table of Contents

Introduction 1

Part One: Red Light — Stop! 2

Chapter 1: His personality 3
  His disposition 3
  His insecurities 4
  Trust issues 6
  Bad boys — what's the attraction? 7
  Moving too soon, too fast 10
  He tries to isolate you from family and friends 12
  Number of children
     (and children's mothers) he has 14

Chapter 2: His smooth moves 17
  Don't believe the hype! 17
  Lines, lines and more lines 18
  Birth control 23
  Signs of STIs 24
  Married and committed men 25
  Listen to what he's telling you 28

Chapter 3: His background 31
  Meeting his family and friends 31
  Interaction with and between his parents 33
  Background checks 34

In a Nutshell 37

Part Two: Yellow Light — Proceed with caution.......40
Chapter 4: His personality 41
  Lack of respect 41
  Smooth talker 42
  If his actions don't match his words...............43
  His money personality 45
  Selfishness....................................47

Chapter 5: His actions............................49
  Is he really interested in *you*?...................49
  He says he loves you too soon 51
  He pressures you to sleep with him 53
  Male and female roles 54
  Mother and son relationship.....................56
  When he's incommunicado 59

Chapter 6: His past 63
  Rebound relationships 63
  Looking at his past relationships 65
  Still living at home? Examine why 66
  Meet his friends and family 68

Chapter 7: Questions to ask myself.................71
  Can I be myself?................................71
  Can I be upfront about my beliefs? 72
  What's my gut telling me? 74
  If he's older, why is he interested in someone my age?..75
  Does he have follow-through?....................77
  Am I settling for him or comparing him to past men?..79
  What do I *know* I can't live with? 82
  Have I asked my man these questions? 84

In a Nutshell....................................89

Part Three: Green Light — Continue to proceed, but keep your eyes open! 90
Chapter 8: His personality 91
  He is honest and respectful......................91
  He appreciates the good and bad of you 93
  He's supportive................................93
  He's responsible 94
  He listens to you...............................95
  He makes you laugh............................98
  He's patient and understanding 99
  He's compassionate 100
  He's trustworthy 101

Chapter 9: His actions..........................105
  You are friends first...........................105
  He lives his life for God.......................106
  He takes his time, but not too much time.........108
  He's ready to head a household 109
  He's in it for the long haul:
     children with special needs..................110
  He puts his family first........................112
  He believes in monogamy 113
  He is a man with a plan 114
  He has a financial plan 116

In a Nutshell..................................119

Conclusion 121

Appendices
  Appendix I: Background check web sites 123
  Appendix II: Negotiable — Non-negotiable chart...125

Recommended Reading List 127

Endnotes 129

Index 131

Introduction

The purpose of this book is to help you avoid common traps men set when dating. Let me stress up front that this book does not describe all men! This is not a book on male bashing. There are a lot of good men out there. I will talk about some of them a bit later. I just want to prepare you for the men who are not so good for you.

You may wonder about the lights on the cover and how they relate to the book. Let me explain.

There are different signs in traffic that teach us how to proceed. You stop if the light is red, proceed with caution or yield at a yellow light and continue moving forward if the light is green. In dating and relationships you can follow similar signals. In this book, I will explain how to avoid hazardous and unhealthy relationships. I will also explore when to stop, when to proceed with caution and when to go — while keeping your eyes open!

I will share personal experiences, mock situations, tips and more. Several topics I cover will come from a Christian perspective. Regardless of what you practice or don't practice, I'm sure you will still gain some insights and be able to apply them to your own life. If I haven't given you enough to ponder, there is a recommended reading list at the end.

So, sit back and get ready because you might read some things even your mother didn't tell you. And whatever you learn — pass it on!

Part One

RED LIGHT – STOP!

I'm sure many of you have met someone and your brain immediately screamed, "Run!" Right? Well, sometimes the signs aren't so obvious.

Let's explore a few areas you may overlook when meeting someone, to help you recognize your next "Red Light" encounter.

His personality

The saying that we shouldn't judge a book by its cover is true and is appropriate when dating. If you only focus on what the man looks like, his walk or his talk, you are missing out on an integral part of who he is. Pay close attention to your man's personality. Here are a few areas you will want to focus on.

His disposition

Does the man you're dealing with seem to have more personalities than a chameleon has colors? If he's moody or his personality is difficult to gauge from one moment to the next, this might be a problem.

The man you're involved with should be emotionally stable. You should not have to walk on eggshells every time you are together. If you find yourself being hesitant to ask questions, speak your mind or just be yourself when you're around him, it's time for you to re-evaluate this relationship. Even if you aren't dating yet, this is not the kind of friendship you want for yourself. Don't base your actions on how he might respond at that moment.

I had a friend like that once.

If we were talking on the phone and he needed to go, no problem. But the minute I ended the conversation first, he got an attitude. There were other occasions where I felt I couldn't ask him something because he didn't like people "questioning him," as he put it, even if it was a simple question out of curiosity.

At one point we stopped communicating altogether because he got mad at me for how I said something. That behavior got old quickly and eventually we had a talk about it. I basically told him that I could not have a friendship where I wasn't comfortable and that our conversation that day would determine if we remained friends or went our separate ways. Our friendship had gone on too long unbalanced.

I named specific times when I didn't feel he treated me like a friend and told him that even if he was upset with me he could let me know and love me anyway. I explained how I expected him to treat me and asked if that was something he could handle.

We did manage to salvage our friendship and we remain in contact today. It's different than before, but as time goes on and we readjust to this new friendship I'm sure we'll be fine. I had to take that first step though, to set the standard for how I would be treated from that point forward.

Be sure to surround yourself with people who care about and value you for who you are, as you are. Look for the same qualities in the men you date.

His insecurities

What are his insecurities? Does he deal with them? Maybe a man you meet tells you he never finished college, but would like to go back. Does he handle that by re-enrolling in school or does he downplay and make snide remarks about your degree?

Of course you don't rub your education in his face or make him feel inferior because he hasn't attained his own degree. However, don't allow him to make you feel insecure about yourself when he's the one with the problem. Dealing with issues does not mean it's okay to pull you down in the process.

A friend of mine, Jackie, met this guy, Tony. They seemed to be pretty compatible, but Tony had a habit that started to bother Jackie after a while.

Jackie kept herself in good shape. She worked out regularly and was conscious about what she ate.

Tony liked to look fit also, but wasn't always willing to put in the work. He would often compare himself to other men he and Jackie would run into while they were out. He would ask her who she thought had better legs, arms, etc. Sometimes Tony would go as far as to accuse Jackie of being interested in guys who were more physically fit than he was, including the ones at the gym where she worked out. It got so bad that Tony tried to demand that Jackie not go to the gym if he wasn't with her, which was hardly ever, since he wasn't committed. Even if Tony did work out more often, it still may not have rid him of his insecurity because he needed to be comfortable with who he was on the inside first.

The problem in this example is that Tony's insecurities began to have a negative effect on Jackie, which ultimately took a toll on their relationship.

Trust issues

Having trust issues is another type of insecurity some men have.

Perhaps the man you're involved with has a hard time trusting women. This could be the result of a previous relationship or possibly stem from witnessing certain behavior by his mother. As helpful as it is to know the root of this behavior, it is not a good idea to excuse the behavior associated with this insecurity.

I dated a young man once who constantly accused me of being interested in other men. He would pressure me to know who was on the other line if I happened to click back over to him and be smiling or laughing. Mind you it was the family phone line, so it could have been anyone. Despite my attempts to convince him that he was the only one I was interested in, the accusations did not stop. I had to end the relationship.

Trust is one of the cornerstones of any good relationship. Some women have allowed themselves to be interrogated and humiliated, all because the man struggled with trust issues. One guy checked his wife's panties whenever she returned home from grocery shopping!

Is this what you want for yourself? It's not cute when your man is always asking where you are or what you're doing. He's not truly concerned when he's wondering who you're talking to every time you pick up the phone or having you check in every time you go someplace. He's not trying to protect you or make sure you arrive safely. He doesn't trust you and that is a problem.

Many times, the person who is accusing you of doing something behind his back is probably doing that very thing behind your back. Trust is not about holding on as tight as you can and squeezing the life out of a person. It's about being able to let go and still be comfortable knowing that person isn't going to intentionally hurt or take advantage of you.

You may think trust issues aren't that bad, but be assured that besides making your life miserable with the accusations, various forms of abuse can result from this insecurity. When you sign up for a relationship with a man who has trust issues, you may end up with more than you bargained for.

Bad boys – what's the attraction?

I'm sure many of you have heard about women being more attracted to the "bad boy" than the "nice guy." But do you know why women have this tendency? And do you know why it's so bad?

Let's talk about it for a moment. I want you to recognize the signs so you can avoid this type of relationship or break the cycle if this describes you.

Here's a story about Wendy and Jason. They met a few years ago at work. Wendy liked the fact that Jason commanded respect from others. He looked tough, acted tougher and people tended to stay out of his way.

Wendy knew if he was her man he would stick up for her. She also liked the adventurous side of Jason. He often rode a motorcycle to work, and when they had company outings or activities, Jason would usually jump out front and show how good he was. Sometimes he'd smoke weed, but he always managed to pass his drug test.

There was this other guy, Sean, who worked there also. He had noticed Wendy a while ago, but Wendy wasn't too interested, said he wasn't her type — too boring, seemed too soft-spoken and kept to himself a lot.

"Nice guy, but no thanks," was what she'd say. Her eyes were on Jason.

Fast-forward six months. Wendy and Jason start dating. Wendy thinks she's found all she's been looking for in Jason. She still works at the same place, but Jason no longer works there because he was fired for insubordination and intimidating a supervisor.

Sean was still there, steadily working his way up in the company. He would come around Wendy more since Jason wasn't there.

Jason began to take out his frustration of always being "misunderstood" on Wendy, criticizing her, pushing her around and eventually hitting her. The guy who started out as a cool, tough guy had started becoming rough with Wendy and she didn't know how to handle it. She began to confide in Sean, who always had a listening ear and tried many times to convince her to leave Jason.

Let's stop here.

Notice how Wendy perceived Jason when they met. She saw his "tough guy" behavior as a good characteristic and thought he'd be a good protector. In reality, his behavior was symptomatic of someone with abusive tendencies — intimidating, confrontational and easily set-off. What Wendy perceived as adventurous traits were actually reckless and egotistic characteristics found in someone who abuses.

When a man thinks he's the most important person and exhibits careless or reckless behavior, he is not considering anyone other than himself. He is always right and if he's wrong it's someone else's fault. Indulging in drugs can also exacerbate behaviors already present.

The traits Wendy was looking for in a man were not wrong. Being with a man who makes you feel protected and secure and has a bit of a wild side is something that attracts many women. The key is to make sure what is perceived is not confused with the reality of the situation. "Bad boys" mimic many of the characteristics women find desirable in a man:

Perception	Reality
Sense of security	Fights often to maintain respect from others
Fun-loving/spontaneous	Engages in reckless behavior
Attracted to you	Has a high sex drive
Buys you nice things	Stakes his claim through money*
Attentive	Possessive

*Be careful with this. If a man is buying you nice, expensive things, he may be using it as a way to claim you as his. He could easily demand you "give him back his stuff" one day, even to the point of taking "his" clothing off of you in public because he got mad at you for something. In his mind, whatever he bought you is still his, so he can take it back whenever he wants. My parents taught me only to accept things I can read, smell and taste, never clothing or anything too costly.

Sometimes it's hard to tell the difference between which behaviors are perceived and what the reality of the situation really is. It's important to take the time and assess the man you're interested in and be honest with yourself about what you're seeing. It is helpful to recognize things about your background that draw you to this kind of guy. I'll discuss this more in detail in later chapters. By doing these things, you can potentially avoid an unhealthy relationship. You may even find that given a chance, that boring "nice guy" has all of the qualities you were looking for in the first place — just in a less in-your-face kind of way.

Moving too soon too fast

A girlfriend of mine had a tendency to meet men who seemed to be on a fast track toward relationships. After speaking to one man on the phone the first time, the guy was already imagining them sitting near the fireplace, with my friend wearing a wedding ring.

Hello? Not only does that exude desperation, but it makes you wonder what else he rushes into without forethought. I'll say this now and you'll see it again throughout the book: Marriage is for mature, responsible people. There's a popular movie titled, *Fools Rush In.* This is true — only fools do rush in. Take time to get to know him and give yourself the opportunity to process before charging full speed ahead.

This same friend met someone else. After the first date, she was "convinced" this was the final stop on the dating train with all signs pointed toward matrimony. Notice the quotations around convinced. My friend admits to being smitten by the young man. She was so swayed by what he said, how he looked, etc., that she overlooked many of the signs that would have led her to the conclusion that this was a "Red Light" relationship. They eventually did marry — and divorced shortly after.

There was yet another suitor who moved so fast, she didn't even know they were dating. Apparently, he picked a date from a time when they went out and that was the day they became a couple. Wouldn't you like to know if you had a boyfriend? It's only fair if all parties involved are aware of this budding relationship!

If you notice things moving too quickly with a man — beware! There's usually a reason he's on this fast track. He may very well be the type who knows what he wants and goes after it with zeal. On the other hand, he can have character flaws he's hoping you won't have time to notice until it's too late.

(Note: It's never too late to get out of an unhealthy relationship, but many women get so invested they feel there's no alternative but to stay.)

Remember the power you have when becoming involved with someone. If things are too fast for you, speak up and slow down. The relationship will only proceed at a pace you approve. It's like a car — as hard as you press the accelerator, the car won't move if it's in Park. Exercise your prerogative to put your relationship in Park or Reverse and discuss your expectations for the relationship.

I remember meeting someone, and things were going great — all except for the fact that this man was moving entirely too fast for my comfort level. After talking we realized that he considered holding hands, snuggling and just being close as things you do as you get to know a person. For me, those were things that weren't done until after you got to know the person.

Basically, his step one was my step three or four. If this was never discussed, imagine the mixed signals that would have been sent. He would have thought I wasn't interested and I would have thought he was moving at freight train speed.

I'm sure many of these examples have made you chuckle and even laugh out loud, but consider the serious side as well and let these stories give you food for thought. People who rush tend to make mistakes and a relationship is not the place for avoidable mistakes.

HE TRIES TO ISOLATE YOU
FROM FAMILY AND FRIENDS

Maybe moving too fast isn't an issue for you. But perhaps you've noticed other things that don't settle well with you. The guy you're with has met your family and friends and knows you're close, but always makes a big deal about how much time you spend together — be it in person or on the phone. Any time you're with him and happen to speak to a friend or someone in your family on the phone, he gets upset. Either he picks a fight every time you hang up or distracts you so much that you end the call early. He may even interrupt and inject himself into the conversation so frequently that what began as a two-way conversation has now become a three-way.

Something else you may have noticed is that he always has a reason you shouldn't spend time with your family or friends but spend it with him instead. He doesn't even want the two of you to hang out with your family or friends together.

You gradually get pulled away from your family and friends and spend all of your time with him. Being in the relationship, you don't or can't see what's going on. Those on the outside looking in can see it as plain as day. He's trying to isolate you and keep you all to himself. It may not seem like such a big deal at first, but your relationship could take a turn for the worse as times goes on.

This type of isolating behavior can be characteristic of someone who is insecure, controlling and abusive. If the relationship starts to turn sour, you won't have anyone to rely on for help because you've slowly, but steadily, lost contact with everyone who was close to you.

There was a story on TV a while back about a woman who ended up marrying a man like I just described. He had her so isolated from family and friends that they relocated and family and friends didn't even know where she was. When he went to work, she had no phone access and he had her locked in her own home! Now this is an extreme case, but it started with him isolating her from her family and friends.

Beware of men who try to do this to you. A man who's interested in you should want to get to know your friends and family just as you should get to know his.

Number of children
(and children's mothers) he has

These days, this question comes up more and more often — how many kids does he have? This is important for a couple of reasons. The number of children he has may be an indicator of how responsible he is.

I once met a man with six children. Only one was the result of marriage and there were several different mothers. This kind of situation should automatically put you on alert. One child because of a slip-up happens to many people. But five?

Did he even bother to be responsible during his sexual encounters or did he act first and think later, not asking if she was using birth control? Does this lack of planning and responsibility carry over into the rest of his life?

Does he take responsibility for his children or allow the mothers to carry the brunt of the weight in raising them?

All of these questions should be considered when you meet a man with several children.

Another thing to consider when meeting a man with several children is that you will have to deal with all of the mothers of these children. We all know the drama that can happen when other mothers are involved. This could go on for years, at least until they turn 18. Is this what you envision for yourself?

Speaking of the mothers, beware of men who tell you they are roommates with the kids' mother, no matter what reason they give you. They're sharing more than the house.

I actually met two men who told me they were living

with the mother of their children as roommates. One said it was because his child had a learning disability. The other man claimed he and his girlfriend had just broken up and she hadn't found a place to live yet. And they both thought I'd be okay with that! Funny enough, both of these men had five children apiece. Under no circumstances should you date a man still living with the mother of his children.

It is possible this type of man has learned from his past, has matured and is making more responsible choices. All of the mothers may end up getting along with you and each other. You won't know until you spend time with him, but do so at your own risk. There's a reason I put this topic in the "Red Light" zone.

His smooth moves

In the last chapter, I talked about personality traits you should be aware of. Now, we're going to delve a bit deeper and discuss some moves he might make that are so smooth you'll completely overlook the warning signs.

DON'T BELIEVE THE HYPE!

Remember my friend who was convinced she'd found her soul mate? Part of the reason was because of what this man told her. Often a man will tell you what you want to hear.

Be careful not to tell everything about yourself at once, giving him an ample selection of things to choose from to make himself sound like your ideal mate. You can share pieces of information about yourself, just make sure he's not parroting your responses to seem like a perfect match.

Here's an example. You say, "I love to go camping!" and he says, "Oh, yeah, me too, the fresh air, being one with nature, blah, blah, blah …" And then you make plans to actually go camping and find out he never went camping; he only watched "Survivor" on T.V. and thought it looked interesting.

It's important not to get caught up in what he says. Look past his words and see if he's really saying something. Take time to truly listen and then ask questions that force him to explain further. We always put on our "best face" when we meet someone. Be ready to hear what he's talking about, while listening to what he's actually telling you.

Don't get caught up like my friend did and fall head over heels just based on what he tells you. Make it a priority to not only talk to him, but meet his family, friends, co-workers and see if the picture he paints lines up with how he lives.

"Talk is cheap," is a common expression, and when it comes to becoming involved with a man, make sure "talk" isn't all you're getting. If a man tells you he has plans to do something, watch his follow-through. Don't allow yourself to be strung along, holding onto the hope that, "This is his year! He might make it happen this time," or thinking, "But he has so much potential!" We all have potential, but we all don't put it to good use.

See if his words and actions line up before you get too involved. Remember, if he's like this now, you can pretty much guarantee it's not going to change.

Lines, lines and more lines

Along the same lines (no pun intended), maybe you've heard some of these before:

- I love you
- What's up tonight? You wanna come over and just chill?
- Can you stay a little longer to talk?
- I'm ready to move to the next level
- I want to be one with you
- I just want to love every part of you

- I've really made a connection with you and I want a deeper connection
- Everybody else is doing it
- Well, we've already done everything else, so we might as well
- I haven't had sex in a year and I'm not sleeping with a lot women so you can trust that I won't hurt you
- You can trust me!
- Let's make the night complete — we've had dinner and a movie
- I've been patient. How long do I have to wait?
- I don't want to have sex with you. I wanna *make love* to you
- I want to please you
- I want to know how it feels to be inside of you

If these don't sound familiar, insert lines you have heard. The point is, he wants S-E-X. Furthermore, he wants to see exactly what he has to say to convince you to have sex with him.

Don't think because you've told him no before that it's over. He *will* ask again (and again), until he gets what he wants. Ladies, if sex is not what you want, don't budge. Not even a little bit. If you give an inch, next thing you know, you'll be flat on your back, wondering how you ended up in that position and how he managed to get your clothes off so fast!

The best way to avoid a compromising situation is to make sure you don't put yourself in places or situations that could lead to sex. Stay in public, well-lit places with other friends. Don't hang out alone at each other's houses. Don't lie down and don't go in his or your bedroom. You have to set your standards and keep them or you will be bulldozed every time.

Okay, let's get back to the lines. Some of them are so corny you might laugh right in his face. But brace yourself for the more subtle ones so you don't get swept up by the romanticism. A man may tell you he loves you and mean it, but if he really cared about you, and knew sex was not on your agenda, he would respect you enough not to dangle the "love" card to convince you to have sex.

What it boils down to, is does he respect you? And not only that, do you respect yourself enough to set the record straight about what you want or don't want to happen — and stick to it? Men can tell when they're making headway and wearing you down. So if one line didn't do it for him, you better believe he's coming back with more artillery. He'll have you feeling so good and get you so hot and bothered that all of your standards will find themselves on the other side of the door while you're getting it on in the bedroom! When it's all over, you have to deal with your conscience. Those same standards you discarded for a moment of pleasure will be harder to keep when the next situation presents itself. And believe me, it will.

As a follower of Jesus Christ, I firmly support abstinence until marriage. This does not mean I have never been faced with these lines before or that I haven't been challenged in this area. But, if you know who you are in Christ, value yourself and guard your heart and mind, you'll have an easier time recognizing these lines for what they are:

GAME — pure, unadulterated game, designed solely to get in your panties and move on. You're worth more than this, ladies. Start seeing yourself as the jewel God created you to be and demand to be handled with care and respect.

Are you dating a man who uses any of these lines to convince you to have sex, and are you feeling pressured? I suggest you take a step back. Maybe you just need to be clear with him about what you will and won't do in your relationship and share how his pressure makes you feel. If he respects you, he'll back off. If he doesn't back off — a clear indicator he doesn't respect or care about you — you must decide if this is the kind of relationship you want to be involved in. Even if he does back off, if your views about sex differ, this situation may arise again.

Perhaps you believe in waiting until marriage to have sex and he doesn't. He may not understand why you want to wait, especially if you've professed love for him, or if you're engaged. Your rejection of sex may be, in his eyes, a rejection of him and that will put a strain on your relationship. Keep the lines of communication open and make whatever changes necessary to avoid compromising your beliefs. If you respect you, he'll have to respect you. And if he doesn't, you'll be so content with yourself that moving on won't be so hard.

One suggestion is to take the pressure off yourself and place the ball in his court. Find ways to counter his lines with responses that stop him in his tracks and make him realize he needs to start seeing you differently. Here are a few examples to give you an idea of what I mean.

He says	You say
"I've really made a connection with you and I want to go deeper."	"Exactly what did you have in mind?" Once you know he's talking about sex: "I think we've connected well too. I am not interested in a sexual relationship, but I'd love for us to continue getting to know one another better."
"Everybody else is doing it."	"I am not everybody else. I'm sure my uniqueness is one thing that attracted you to me. Choosing to not follow the crowd on this just gives you another reason to like me."
"You can trust me!"	"I am not interested in having sex because I have chosen to abstain. It's not even about trust. But since you brought it up, can I trust you to respect that?"
"Let's make the night complete — we've already had dinner and a movie."	"My evening is already complete. I do not need to have sex to round it out. I'm sure we can find something else to do. If not, I'm okay with calling it a night and heading home."
"We've already done everything else, so we might as well."	"I shouldn't have gone as far with you as I did. And just because we did some things doesn't mean it has to lead to sex. I don't want a sexual relationship, and it looks like we might need to go separate ways so I can follow what I believe."

See ladies? Just like he puts thought into how he'll get you out of your panties, you need to be prepared to keep them on. Ultimately, I still go back to my original advice. If he really respects you, he won't pressure you to do anything you are not comfortable with.

Birth control

If you decide you want your relationship to include sex, is he willing to discuss birth control? As I said before, marriage is for mature, responsible people. The same applies to babies. If you aren't ready to raise a child, the two of you should be abstaining or having talks about birth control and taking steps toward using it. Don't let him talk you into not using anything.

A friend of mine dated a guy who didn't believe in using birth control of any kind. He tried to use the withdrawal method. Well, withdrawal is 96 percent effective if always done right and only 73 percent effective when not always done correctly.[1] So, you can already guess what happened. She got pregnant and the first thing the guy wanted to do was "withdraw" from the situation and leave her to raise the child on her own.

Ladies, you are responsible for making decisions that best suit you. There are various forms of birth control available. Some have more side effects than others, but rest assured, next to a baby you weren't ready to raise, those side effects pale in comparison.

Talk with your family doctor about which method of birth control to use. You may be apprehensive about speaking to your doctor, but if you're mature enough to have sex, be mature enough to speak with someone who has all the facts. Listening to your girlfriends or your man on a topic this important could land you in a situation you aren't prepared to deal with.

Signs of STIs

Another item on your list of "Things to consider now that I'm having sex," is Sexually Transmitted Infections, commonly known as STIs.

If you think having a baby is the only thing you don't want, think again. STI symptoms and side effects can be long-lasting and in some cases, incurable, causing death. Make sure to look for signs of STIs on yourself and your partner. Only asking if he has any STIs is not enough. Check for yourself. Many of you may be familiar with the song by Teddy Pendergrass that talks about turning off the lights before being intimate. Now is not the time for that. Turn on the lights, so you don't miss something important.

Be aware that STIs are not limited to genitalia — you can contract them orally and anally. It's also good to know that all STI symptoms don't readily appear, and may carry no symptoms at all. And keep in mind that all types of birth control do not protect against STIs.

As an extra precaution, get tested together and vow not to engage in any type of sexual behavior until you've both been cleared. If he tells you he's already been tested, see the records for yourself. People lie. While no lie is good, the ramifications of a lie of this nature can have life-altering effects. And if he accuses you of not trusting him, don't allow that to sway you. Your life is at stake.

Having sex is a big decision and should be handled as such. As much as I promote abstinence, I can't overlook the fact that abstinence won't be the choice some of you make. Consequently, I decided to at least give you a heads-up in a few areas so you know what you're walking into and can make intelligent decisions.

Married and committed men

Another man who will tell you what you want to hear is a man who's already taken. Yes, I said it — a man who has a wife or girlfriend, but is looking for a little something on the side. Let me state emphatically that a man in a committed relationship, be it married or exclusively dating, is off limits! No exceptions to this rule. God will not bless you with someone else's man. I'm sure some of you have found yourselves in the position of the "other woman" and I know women who have too. So let's take a few moments to expose and dispel some of the myths you may find yourself rationalizing.

Perhaps you've met a man who seems to have it all together and you two hit it off right away. As you get to know him you find out he's married, but — surprise, surprise! — it's not a happy union. He then proceeds to share details about their relationship and give reasons why he's not happy.

He may say things like, "I don't know what happened. She's not like she used to be. She doesn't cook, clean, pay attention to me or look like she did before." Or, "I'm only staying because of the kids. We don't have a real relationship; I mean we don't even sleep together anymore. We're more like roommates."

These stories are designed to play on your emotions and evoke sympathy so you'll go along with his plans. No man in a committed relationship should be telling you details of his relationship. But he will and you'll want to take his side because you can't believe his wife would be that way. If you've known him for a while, it's even easier to take his side. You simply won't understand how she could not want to be with such a good man. Your nurturing nature kicks in and you jump to the rescue. You offer an ear and a shoulder and before you know it, your friendship has taken on characteristics of a relationship. He claims, "You understand me so much better than my wife does," and "I feel so comfortable when I talk to you. My wife and I never talk like this."

Remember ladies, there are two sides to every story, actually three — his side, her side and the truth. You don't live with them, so no matter how dismal he makes his relationship seem, you don't know the whole story. And even if you do, this is still not cause for you to get involved with a man in a married or committed relationship. Ladies, you are worth more than this!

You were not created to settle for less than God's best for you. Becoming involved with a married man is not God's best. Don't sell yourself short. Maybe your self-image is not where it should be and attention from any man, married or single, makes you feel wanted. You will get to a point when you'll feel good about who you are and what you have to offer. Engaging or remaining in a relationship with a man already committed will only delay your progress.

Why?

Well, he tells you all these things about how great you are and how happy you make him feel and that you're so beautiful. Yet, he's still with his wife or girlfriend. Talk about a kick to the self-esteem! You *are* great, you *are* beautiful and you *will* make a man happy — just not this man. He belongs to someone else. Nothing you do, short of humiliating yourself and cutting off your blessings, will change that.

When you choose to involve yourself with a man in a committed relationship, his family is also affected. How do you think he finds all this time to be with you? By lying to his family. Time spent with you is time subtracted from his family. Money he spends on you is money he didn't spend on his family.

Please don't put yourself in this situation. Too many people end up hurt, and what's worse is that you may find out everything this man told you is a lie. You are too intelligent to be made to look like a fool.

So, here are some suggestions to help you avoid falling into this trap.

If you meet a man and find out he's married or in a committed relationship, walk away. Better yet, run! Lose his number and make it clear that you do not want to communicate with him again. There is nothing for him to explain and he doesn't need to see you one more time for closure. By this time, you are already attracted to each other, so further contact will only make it harder to break away.

If he tells you he's getting a divorce, tell him you will not be waiting around for that to happen. If he indeed gets divorced and he's really interested in you, he'll find you. Divorce is a trying time and he may tell you he needs someone to talk to. You cannot be that person because, as I stated earlier, the attraction is already there, so you can't "just" be a sounding board. Being his friend is not an option. Your feelings will grow with each conversation and you'll be in an unhealthy situation.

You have to guard yourself from being pulled into harmful situations.

If you are involved with a man in a committed relationship and you are not the girlfriend or wife, you are setting yourself up for disappointment and hurting many people in the process. Pain caused by these affairs can have long-lasting effects on you as well as on the man's family. When you have a good man and are in a "Green Light" relationship, you wouldn't want another woman to come along and threaten what you've worked so hard to achieve. Don't be that woman for someone else.

Listen to What He's Telling You

In the world of spoken word poetry, when you say something profound that the audience likes, they'll say, "Rewind!" which translates into "Go back and repeat what you just said, because that was deep!"

So let me rewind and reiterate the point that it's important to listen to what he's telling you. Don't get in such a habit of looking past his words that you miss important things he's trying to tell you about himself.

For example, a girlfriend of mine met a man who was showing signs of being in the "Red Light" zone. When they would talk he would proclaim that he was lazy. Now, I just told you we tend to put on our best face when we first meet someone, right? If this is what he's saying from the beginning, it won't get any better.

Here's another example.

I met a man who had excellent ideas, plans for the future and even blueprints for various projects. Looks promising so far? Well, I quickly learned, mostly from what he said and some observation, that all of his plans would only be a reality if someone else executed them. He explicitly told me once, in response to an idea I presented, that if I would do all the legwork and get it started, he'd jump right in. His inability to step out on his own and "turn blueprints into buildings" was limiting his potential and future success. Whoever dates or marries him will probably have to take on the role of "initiator" in several areas of their relationship in order for things to get done. But it won't come as a surprise because he spelled it out in the beginning.

Maybe the new guy you meet tells you he doesn't want to have a baby, but you do. Please don't make the mistake of thinking he's going to change his mind. Just because he's good with kids or adores your daughter, this is not a sign that he wants more. He may even have kids of his own but may not want more. If you proceed in this relationship, rest assured you will most likely be disappointed after all the time, energy and love you've invested and he still doesn't want more children. Take a moment and recall your first few dates. Didn't he tell you that in the beginning?

If he's telling you he's lazy, sloppy, doesn't like to work, isn't into exercise, doesn't want kids, etc., believe it. And thank God you're finding out now.

You're not going to change him, so don't have fantasies that once you're together you can influence him with your sense of order, your healthy eating habits, your workout regimen, your maternal instincts, etc. It ain't happening! He is who he is and he's not going to change unless he wants to. So, listen to what he's telling you, accept it and if you don't like it, move on to someone who is more compatible.

His background

As women, we tend to trust easily. When it comes to dating someone, be careful. Don't believe everything a man tells you. These days, the world is crazy. With so many ways to re-create yourself, you need to be sure the man is really who he claims to be. Do some investigative work on your own. Dig as deeply as you have to, both personally and professionally, to ensure you're not being duped.

MEETING HIS FAMILY AND FRIENDS

Previously I mentioned the importance of getting to know his family and friends. Make time and take opportunities to observe how he interacts with them. Do they truly like him or just tolerate him? Does he have many friends? If so, is he close to a few of them or more of a socialite with no lasting ties? If he doesn't have many friends, find out why.

Maybe the man you are with isn't thrilled about you meeting his family or friends. There could be several reasons why he feels this way, but in order to have a well-rounded view of him, you need to meet those he's closest to. Early in the relationship, this may not happen, but if things are getting serious, it is imperative you've met the people who've had the greatest effect on his life.

And, take note when friends and family tell you things

about your man. They've known him longer than you, so unless they have a personal vendetta against him or want to date you themselves, pay attention to what they're telling you. Everything they tell you may not surface or come to pass and people can change. Just don't be so naïve and gullible that you walk into a situation blind when you've been forewarned.

Take the information given and store it. Don't run back to him with the laundry list of what was said, either. If it's true, you've shown your hand and now he has a chance to alter his behavior. Maintain your upper hand and continue to keep your eyes open. You'll know soon enough if what you heard has merit.

Remember, although we all strike out on our own paths in life, the relationships we form growing up play a large part in who we become — or don't — and influence many aspects of our lives.

For example, if a man had a father who was an alcoholic, and although the son didn't drink, he still may exhibit symptoms of a "dry alcoholic" (i.e., exaggerated self-importance, grandiose behavior, a rigid, judgmental outlook, impatience, childish behavior, irrational rationalization, projection, overreaction).[1]

If he wasn't shown a lot of physical affection growing up, he may not be as comfortable being "touchy-feely" with you. Maybe he was an only child. He may show signs of selfishness or may enjoy longs periods of quiet. Perhaps he's one of many children and felt he was never heard. So now, he talks incessantly and is always vying for attention. Some of these characteristics can be picked up in conversation, but to have a firsthand view of how he is around others is priceless.

Interaction with and between his parents

One important interaction to watch for is between him and his father and mother. Being able to observe this interaction will most likely clue you in on how he feels women should be treated and, more particularly, how he'll treat you.

Does he show the utmost respect to his mom, or is he rude and disrespectful? Do you notice him brushing her off and treating her as if she's insignificant or a nuisance he wishes would go away?

What about how his dad treats his mother? Does he value her or merely tolerate her presence? Is he abusive toward her? Remember abuse can be more than physical. Unless he just doesn't care, you probably won't ever see him hit her. But abuse can be mental and emotional as well. He may never put a finger on her, but he may put her down, cause her to be humiliated in public or treat her with such disdain that if there was a hole nearby she'd crawl inside and hibernate.

Look out for even the subtle behavior and decide if this is how you'd want to be treated. Although your man may be nothing like his father, keep in mind this is what he's witnessed his whole life. If he's like his dad, he may exhibit similar characteristics. Conversely, if he didn't approve of how his mom was treated he'll flee in the opposite direction and treat women as the queens and princesses they are.

Background checks

Observing and interacting with friends and family is great but may not always be possible. Even if it is, you still may not get all of the facts. This is when I'd recommend a background check. Your first thought might be, "It's not that serious!" These days, yes it is.

A relative of one of my friends did a background check on a man she was involved with and discovered he was wanted for fraud. When she confronted him about it, he was shocked she'd found out.

I had another friend of mine in Washington State who had just begun dating a young man. He told her his job in Alaska required quite a bit of traveling, so he could be gone several days at a time or even a few weeks, depending on the rotation. Having lived in Alaska before, she knew that was likely, so she didn't think anything of it. She happened to talk to a few friends who worked for the same company and some of the things her guy was telling her were no longer adding up. After doing a bit of research and checking his employment status during a background check, she learned that her man did not work for that company at all. Moreover, his actual job was not even in Alaska and did not require that much travel. After an ugly confrontation she learned that all of his traveling was to be with his family in another state! Who knows what story he told his family.

Unless you ask all the right questions, and sometimes even when you do, you won't get all of the information. I remember meeting this guy and we were getting to know each other. I asked him had he been to jail before and he told me no. The way he answered was a little suspect, so I went further and asked if he'd been in prison, to which he responded he had. Things like that, where he knew what I was asking and he chose to be legalistic and only answer what I asked instead of being forthcoming, is what I'm talking about.

This is where you have to be careful. The man you date should be honest and upfront, but just in case he's not, one way to help yourself is by conducting a background check if you feel the need. Appendix I lists various web sites to help you get started.

The good news is background checks aren't terribly expensive. A basic check can be free (very limited information).[2] More detailed checks can range anywhere from a $9.95/month membership for a month of unlimited membership access[3] to $79.95.[4] A basic background check can provide you with the following information:

- Full name
- Age
- Current address and address history
- Phone number
- Bankruptcies
- Tax liens
- Civil judgments
- Lawsuits
- State criminal search[5]

You may feel doing a background check means you don't trust him, and to a degree, you don't. Between internet dating and meeting strangers off the street, you have no idea who you're dealing with. And, if this is someone you're considering dating seriously or marrying, having all of the facts will help you make an informed decision.

Even if the person you are with is not a stranger, you'd be surprised at how well some women *didn't* know their men. Remember the murderers, child molesters, rapists and kidnappers (Ted Bundy, Son of Sam, Charles Manson, etc.)? Most of them had wives who didn't know about their "dark" side. So don't be fooled.

Do as much homework as you need to feel comfortable in moving forward with any man you encounter. In some instances, it could mean the difference between life and death.

In a Nutshell

I've probably left you in a somber mood from the last chapter, but that's not necessarily a bad thing. Since this part focused on "Red Light" situations, it's only fitting you have some eye-openers to help you recognize your own "Red Light" encounters.

Many of us tend to enter into "Red Light" relationships for one of three reasons. We were never taught what to look out for; we enjoy the drama and unpredictability; or we haven't taken the time to heal, self-validate and self-improve.

I'll speak to the last point.

You are the person who knows you best. And you are probably the only person who is always going to want the best for you. When you find yourself on the other side of a relationship, hurting, you need to take the required time to fully heal before committing yourself to the next new person. If you do not take the time you need you will most likely end up in another "Red Light" relationship or ruin a good "Yellow Light" or "Green Light" relationship because of too much baggage.

Healing will be different for each of us. It may mean seeing a counselor to help you identify unhealthy traits in men you seem drawn to. It may mean taking a hiatus from men for a while so you can reconnect with yourself. Reconnecting with yourself includes self-improvement. Find hobbies that interest you. Develop some new friendships. Open yourself up to new experiences. Exercise for physical and emotional well-being.

All of these self-improvement suggestions will help you feel so much better about yourself and provide opportunities for self-validation.

You need to get a life and live it! That way you won't be so tempted to fall head-over-heels with the first man who says you're beautiful because you feel good about yourself inside and out. A man who travels won't seem so exotic and worldly and entice you with his stories because you've been several places yourself and have stories of your own. I am not suggesting you have it so together you can no longer see the benefit of having a man because you can do everything yourself. However, you should be comfortable in your own skin. Get to know and love who you are. Validate yourself. Make time for yourself.

Do these things, so if you find yourself encountering a "Red Light" situation you can walk away without losing a chunk of self-worth in the process.

Remember what the red light tells you: Stop! Beware! Danger! Hazard! Warning! Lights, bells and whistles should be going off in your head in "Red Light" situations.

I would like you to take a moment to go back over each chapter and think about the man in your life. Do any parts of his personality, smooth moves or background cause you to think you should go running with arms flailing? If so, now's the time to take that step back and re-evaluate your reasons for being in the relationship. Once you do, you'll probably be single again, wondering what your next relationship will be like. This is an okay place to be. Now you're ready to explore the next part, Yellow Light: Proceed with Caution.

Part Two

YELLOW LIGHT — PROCEED WITH CAUTION

You know how when you're driving and come to an intersection with a flashing yellow light? As you move forward, you look to the left and the right, make sure it's safe and then proceed. You don't just plow ahead, giving little attention to your surroundings, right? This sense of caution should carry over when considering a potential relationship.

Something you should understand about "Yellow Light" relationships is that sometimes a good heart-to-heart talk can help clear things up and move you toward a "Green Light" relationship. These relationships may require a bit more maintenance initially, but unlike a "Red Light" relationship, "Yellow Light" relationships have the potential to succeed.

His personality

Men in "Red Light" relationships can have obvious personality flaws, but there are subtleties you can easily disregard in the "Yellow Light" stage. Rather than ignoring them, those "little things" you notice should be brought to the table. Let's explore five areas where some questionable personality traits may appear.

LACK OF RESPECT

Maybe you're in a relationship and things are progressing, but something just isn't quite right. He seems to treat you alright, but sometimes you notice he brushes you off or doesn't show up at places on time. When he does get there, his attitude is one of nonchalance. These are signs of his lack of respect toward you. At no time should your desires or feelings be disregarded. Even if he doesn't agree with you, he can express that respectfully.

Another way he may not respect you is by not blatantly disrespecting you but by convincing you of things.

For example, a friend of mine wanted to go to a specific restaurant for her birthday. Her date didn't want to go there, so he convinced her to eat at a different place. He casually suggested his choice was better and that he was more informed since he was from that area.

Or maybe you have plans to go to law school and he influences you to drop those plans and pursue a business degree, citing all the reasons business is better than law.

Some men are so subtle you may not even realize he's convinced you to change your mind until it's done. Be alert to this maneuver. He's not respecting what you want and just offering alternatives. He's swaying you to change your mind right under your nose and making you think it's your idea.

If you notice this happening, don't automatically assume the relationship is doomed. This is where communication comes in. Take time and express your concerns to your man and share your idea of how you want things to progress. Be clear and concise. If he's receptive and his behavior changes, great! Your "Yellow Light" may become a "Green Light" at some point.

If he ignores your request and thinks you're blowing things out of proportion, this is a good time to re-evaluate the relationship and decide if it's the best one for you.

Smooth talker

Maybe the man you're dating is a smooth talker. He makes everything appear okay even when it's not. At times, you may discover "white lies" he's told to cover up something going on with him.

If other areas in your relationship are going well, take a moment to examine this problem area. It's possible he wants to impress you by telling you what he thinks you want to hear. While *you* know you'd be much more impressed with the truth, perhaps he thinks his smooth talking is the best way not to disappoint you. Maybe this is completely off the mark and he's trying to see what he can get away with.

Either way, you need to talk to him and let him know your expectations of honesty in all circumstances. If he can't live up to that expectation, can you live with that? If your answer is no, make a change and wait for someone who knows that the way to impress and get closer to you is by telling the truth.

A relationship full of lies (even small white ones) is like a building with missing bricks. Neither will sustain large amounts of stress or strain. No matter how you build it, the building will eventually crumble because it — just like the relationship — is unstable.

IF HIS ACTIONS DON'T MATCH HIS WORDS

Now let's say you've met someone who talks a good game, but his actions rarely match his words. Everything you do is with baited breath because you don't know if there will actually be follow-through. This might happen to you quite often. If it does, there is a problem.

How can you proceed in a relationship where your man tells you he'll do something that never gets done? It could start with something simple like him telling you he'll call you Monday and you don't hear from him until Thursday. It could end up with him telling you he's going to pay a bill and it's still sitting on his desk a month later!

Here is another example of when communication is key.

Everyone does not have the same level of consideration for others. Though this seeming lack of follow-through is an issue for you, this may be how he is with everyone he encounters. Let him know this is a problem for you.

Perhaps you can tell him not to make promises to call if he can't keep his word. Or, instead of waiting indefinitely for him to get back to you, if he wants to make plans, tell him to call you only after he has all the details worked out. Explain that you have things to do and can't sit, wait and wonder if his plans will actually come to pass.

Earlier I said that maybe he just doesn't hold the same views about being in touch and following through. Something else to consider is how interested he really is. Let's not take for granted that some men don't have a clue. No offense to men, but I've been speaking truth until now, no need to stop!

However, sometimes his lack of being in touch is the only way he knows to let you know that you are not as high on his priority list as he is on yours. Be honest with yourself so you don't waste time being interested in a man who isn't even thinking about you. Generally, if a man is interested, you won't have to guess.

The point? Don't get stuck in a cycle of "he loves me, he loves me not" every time he calls, or doesn't. Communicate, see where he's coming from and proceed accordingly.

Maybe you remember the book (now a movie) titled, *He's Just Not That Into You*. Classic cases are shown of women who don't realize the men they've set their hearts on are completely uninterested. One of the main characters makes a fool of herself trying to gain a guy's attention until she finally realizes her worth and builds up her self-esteem. If you haven't read the book or seen the movie, check it out.

His money personality

This next topic can be a little touchy and is the number one reason many couples break up — money. It's important to know how your man spends his money and make sure you're on the same page financially. I once went out with a man who practically gave away money to impress me. Apparently he thought the more money he flashed the more I'd like him. That approach didn't quite do the trick. What he didn't know was how frugal I am and that I was looking to be impressed by his personality, not his cash. Being of one accord financially will eliminate so many headaches from your relationship.

Does the man you're with budget?

Save?

Spend impulsively?

These are questions worth investigating before the relationship gets too serious. If indeed you don't see eye-to-eye, your "Yellow Light" season is the perfect time to hash things out.

Does your man pay his bills on time?

Is he in debt?

By how much and what kind?

One young lady visited a potential boyfriend at his home. From glancing around (glancing, not snooping, ladies — the stuff was lying around! Don't get any crazy ideas!) she could see offers for credit cards on the table. That was an immediate clue that his credit was decent, which probably meant he paid his bills on time.

On the other hand, a different woman visited a man's

home and all of his bills were stacked on the kitchen table and some of them were past-due. Needless to say, he didn't make the cut. If he's doing this now, why expect it to be different later? This is the time when he's supposed to be putting his best foot forward to impress you. This might be as good as it gets.

Ladies, I urge you to pay attention to these things. You may think money is only one aspect of your relationship, but that's just not true. Money becomes involved when raising kids, buying (and keeping) your house and car, going on trips, paying for college, spending money for all the "extras" you might want and having an emergency fund. Don't think for a moment you can have a successful relationship without ever discussing money.

Here are some other questions to consider.

Who budgets better? That person should probably take care of the bills, while including the other person.

What does his credit look like? Picture this: Everything has to be put in your name and you can no longer afford to buy the things you want — things you could afford while single — because you're busy paying off his debt. As in love as you think you are, you might fall out of love faster than you fell in!

Are either of you "savers" or do you both spend money as soon as you get it? Not having a financial plan, goals or any clue of how you want your money to work for you is a sure recipe for disaster.

Also, make sure *you* are financially sound before getting involved with someone. Don't bring your financial baggage and not expect him to have any of his own. Communicate about your finances and financial expectations and if you're headed toward marriage, come to some joint decisions before you say, "I do."

I'll talk more about having a financial plan in the "Green Light" section.

Selfishness

Here's another sticky topic — selfishness.

We are all selfish to a point, but being selfish can interfere with your relationship. Do you notice that the man you're interested in seems selfish? When you plan to go out to eat and you don't agree on the place, what happens if you decide on your choice? Is he cool with it or does he sulk and complain, constantly berating and comparing your choice to his?

"See if we'd gone to the restaurant I picked, we'd already be eating right now, not standing in line waiting for a table." Or "We'll probably have to split an appetizer since the prices are so high here."

Is there ever compromise? Do you feel you have to go along with what he wants to keep the peace? Does he sabotage situations to get his way?

For example, he really doesn't want to go to church with you, but agrees anyway. He takes his sweet time getting ready so you arrive late and have to sit in the overflow, knowing good and well you hate being late and can't stand sitting in overflow!

You can't say he didn't go, but he has made sure you knew he didn't really want to be there and tried to ruin your good time in the process.

I know some of you are thinking this is a "Red Light" situation. I'll admit it's borderline, but let's dive a little deeper. Depending on how he was raised (spoiled), he may be used to getting his way and is trying the same manipulative tricks on you that he used with his parents. He may be fully aware of what he's doing but may not even realize where it stems from.

If this is someone you truly care about, take the time to let him know his behavior bothers you. Use plenty of "I" statements, expressing how his actions make you feel.

Hopefully the two of you can discuss what compromise means in your relationship and develop more effective ways to communicate when you don't really want to do something. Be careful not to bow out of everything, especially the things that matter most to the other person. In a relationship, your goal should be to please your partner. If you both keep that in front of you, selfishness should not be an issue.

His actions

When you look at a man's actions, often you can get a very good idea about where he's coming from and how you fit in. You should still read between the lines, not taking everything at face value. Remember not to read *so* far between the lines that you're seeing things that aren't really there.

IS HE REALLY INTERESTED IN *YOU*?

When you're with a guy make sure he's truly interested in *you* — your dreams, likes and dislikes, perspective, etc. Now you don't want to go on and on ad nauseam about yourself until his eyes glaze over. However, when you do have a conversation or do things together, pay attention to how much he engages.

When you talk, can you get a complete thought out or does he overtalk you or steer the conversation back to himself? Is he only, or mostly, in touch with you when he needs or wants something but is unavailable when you have a need?

Does he know what matters to you and respond accordingly?

For example, I don't care for stuffed animals as gifts and I make a point of telling people I date. So when I receive them from a man, I know he isn't really interested in what I like or don't — he just went out and bought something without actually considering me.

Does he really care about what you think or how you feel, or just enjoy being seen with you?

He may take you a lot of places, introduce you to everyone dear to him and shower you with everything you could ever want. This may sound like you've found heaven on earth, but what lies behind his actions? He might enjoy buying you nice things so you look better as the trophy on his arm. Make sure you don't become his newest "flavor of the month" and get discarded when the next pretty young thing comes along.

Also, be mindful that he's not only keeping you around because of what you can do for him. Perhaps you know people he needs to meet in order to further his career. That may be why he sought you out in the first place. He could say he likes you, but really only likes the dollar signs attached to your name. Be careful you're not being used for what you look like or what you have. You want to be confident that this man is into you for who you are.

Another thing to keep in mind is that he may not really care what you have or who you know. He may just want to be with *someone* and that someone could be you or anyone else. One way to tell is to ask him what he likes about you or what attracted you to him. If he can't come up with anything or says something generic, he hasn't taken the time to really get to know you at all. You are not expendable. Make sure *you* are who he wants.

His actions will clearly show if he's interested in you or the idea of being with you. If he shows signs of not being truly interested in you, it's time to speak up. Perhaps he doesn't realize the signals he's sending out. You bringing it to his attention may be the jumpstart he needs to get his act together. It's possible he isn't really interested at all and is just taking advantage of the benefits of the relationship until it dissolves, which it should, once you realize how much you're worth.

The bottom line is that you are a woman of value and before proceeding in the relationship you need to be sure he sees and appreciates the jewel that you are.

He says he loves you too soon

Maybe the man you're with is wonderful and things are going well. You've only been dating a short time and he recently told you he loves you. Is it too soon? Well, as with many things, it depends. With men, things are usually pretty straightforward. It's the timeless principle of "he sees, he likes, he conquers." He knows what he wants and he goes after it. Maybe it doesn't take him that long to know he loves you and he's not apprehensive about letting you know. If this is the case, revel in it.

I must also caution you to the other possibility of an early "I love you." Sometimes men say they love you because they know it will prick your emotions and allow them better access to what they want to get from you (i.e., your money, sex, etc.) You may find yourself paying his bills and letting him drive your car, all because he "loves" you.

Don't think it doesn't happen. I have had men tell me about how they have this woman or that woman paying their phone or cable bill and don't think anything of it. And when that woman comes to her senses, he can easily find some other woman gullible enough to do it for him. Don't be lulled into this. *You* will end up broke and looking foolish, not him. Love yourself first, so that if and when he declares his love, his "I love you" won't supersede the love you have for yourself and have you ready to do backflips to please him!

The other possibility of him telling you he loves you early could be that he's needy or insecure. He may cling to you closer than plastic wrap and do anything for you. This may seem ideal and he might actually be a great guy. However, the early "I love you" and the clinginess are signs he's not feeling too confident about himself and needs you to validate him.

I knew someone like this. He was really sweet, quite interested in me and wanted to be around me as often as possible. When he did come around I wasn't out of his sight or too far from arm's reach for very long. After a while it began to bother me, but I couldn't figure out why.

It wasn't until years later that I learned more about his childhood. It became clear that he hadn't experienced love the way a child should. As a result, he sought love from other sources, namely, relationships with women. The insecurity he felt about himself translated into a need to feel loved by someone else and the clingy behavior was exhibited as a result of those feelings. This didn't change the fact that he was a terrific catch — he's currently married with children.

Men who show signs of neediness and emotional insecurity aren't all bad and you don't necessarily have to flee from them. Just be aware that this could explain some of the behaviors you're observing and help you handle it better should you decide to proceed in the relationship.

He pressures you to sleep with him

If you've made it to a "Yellow Light" relationship, unless the two of you have agreed and are following through on not having sex before marriage, this issue will come up time and time again. Where do you stand? Are you firm in your stance about sex or could it change depending on the guy or situation? Whatever you decide, you have to be able to live with it, so choose wisely. It's easier said than done, I know, but a decision still must be made.

If things are going well in the relationship, naturally he's going to want to take it to the next level. What if you don't? Are you willing to leave the relationship if you're feeling pressured?

One of my friends dated a young man who told her that he considered sex to be part of the relationship and expected it to be included if they were going to date. It wasn't something she was accustomed to, but because she really liked him and saw relationship potential she agreed to have sex while dating him. They eventually married and seem to be doing well. Does she regret being involved sexually before marriage? Only she knows the answer to that.

Her circumstances do not determine what you should do. Just because he's a great guy doesn't mean he's the guy for you, especially if you find yourself compromising your convictions to please him. You are not married to this man so *you* are your first priority.

And think about this. What happens if it doesn't work out? You have gone against your principles and now have the guilt to deal with. When the next man comes along will it be the same thing? Don't put your convictions on the shelf because you're being pressured.

If he's really a decent guy, perhaps you can discuss this area and come up with alternatives that you can both agree on. Sometimes men are used to having sex while dating, though it doesn't mean they're not open to something new. Set boundaries together so you are both comfortable within the limitations. Also, continue to communicate.

If what you first talked about needs some tweaking, tweak. Relationships are ever-evolving so it makes sense that feelings and expectations will change as you get to know one another better. If he's unwilling to compromise then you have to decide if this is a relationship you want to continue to be a part of or if you need to sever ties and move on.

Male and female roles

If this was the 1950s I probably wouldn't even be discussing this, but it's the new millennium and things have changed. For the most part, gone are the days of Ward and June Cleaver. If your man is still talking male and female roles this could be a sign of future problems. This may not be a situation that requires fleeing, but you definitely want to consider a few things.

First, does he think there are only certain things a man or woman is capable of? For example, it's the woman's job to cook is a common thought. This may be okay with you at first because you like to cook. But what happens when you get sick or you're working and he's not? Are you still the only one cooking? Why can't this responsibility be shared?

Here's another one. It's the man's job to take care of the finances. Suppose he's no good at budgeting and you are more qualified? Would he have a problem with you taking responsibility for the household finances?

Relationships require a team effort, and male and female roles should not get in the way of running an efficient household. Maybe you alternate cooking by night or who gets home first. The best budgeter leads the finances but it's a joint effort. You both eat so you both do the dishes. Or maybe you wash and he dries. Figure out what works for you based on your circumstances not based on roles established years ago.

Be aware when your conversation turns to male and female roles while dating. This could indicate he's not very flexible but rather rigid and unyielding in some situations. He may be very old fashioned and believe you have a place and should stay in it. It could also just be the way he was raised and how he saw his mother and father interact and adopted that belief for himself. Whichever scenario is true for him doesn't matter. You only need to know if it's going to work for you in your relationship.

Pay attention to other areas in his life to see how his view of male and female roles affects the rest of his life.

Are you treated like his equal? Is what you say dismissed if he feels it's beyond your realm of knowledge? Does he have expectations of you just because you're a woman (you take care of the inside of the house and kids and he'll work and pay bills)? Is your input appreciated or does he feel you're overstepping your bounds in the relationship if you share your opinion? Should you work outside of the home or does he expect you to quit your job once you're married?

Again, his feelings are not deal breakers but you need to be aware of what you're signing up for. If you are in agreement, great! If not, now's the time to walk because his beliefs aren't going to change.

Mother and son relationship

I mentioned your man's relationship with his mother in Chapter Three, but I want to go a bit deeper and in a slightly different direction.

How a man treats his mother is something you want to keep in mind. Often, this gives you a clue as to how he views women and how he's going to treat you. There are some exceptions but generally this is the case.

Your man may talk about his mother all the time but make sure you take the time to watch how they interact. Get to know her for yourself so you have a more well-rounded perspective.

Does your man give his mother the utmost respect? Does he treat her like a queen — open doors for her, take over a task so she can get off her feet, show genuine affection, speak to her in a loving manner, even when frustrated with her, talk about her with reverence even when she's not around? These are behaviors you should look out for.

If he exhibits these behaviors with consistency, the same traits will most likely carry over to your relationship.

While all of these characteristics are good I'm sure you've heard the term "mama's boy," right? Outside of a relationship this can be cute. In a relationship, it can be a whole different story.

You want your man to dote on his mother and treat her well. However, you need him to know how to balance the relationship with his mom and his relationship with you, especially once you start dating seriously.

In Genesis, there's a passage that talks about a man leaving his mother and father and cleaving to his wife. As your relationship progresses and you consider marriage you have to know you will become his number one priority and not take a backseat to his mother. It's great when a man has a close relationship with his mother but you should never be neglected so he can do something for her.

For example, suppose you and your man are out to dinner. His mom calls and tells him she needs him to do something for her. It could wait until later, is not life-threatening and there's no real rush to get it done. Instead of telling his mom he's having dinner with you and make arrangements to do it later he jumps up like it's an emergency and ends the date early. He takes you home so he can help his mom. If he's really bad, he tells you to call a girlfriend for a ride home so he can get to his mother quicker!

This type of behavior can get old quickly and clearly shows he hasn't established the proper boundaries in his relationship with his mother.

If this is not addressed while dating it *will* enter into

the marriage. And like with any marriage, behaviors you dislike will be magnified once you say, "I do" because you're constantly around that person versus when you just went out on dates.

Does this sound like the dating relationship you're in? Can you imagine what this could look like once you're married? What about when you have kids? If what I've mentioned describes the relationship your man has with his mother, don't lose hope! Now is the time to sit down, discuss it and together come up with ways he can still be close to his mother while respecting your relationship. Once he understands the strain it's putting on your relationship he'll adjust his behavior and begin to set those boundaries with his mother.

(As a side note, anytime there are issues between him and his family, let *him* be the one to speak up. This is not your role, as you could end up knee-deep in a situation and ruin whatever relationship you've established with his family. Let him be out front. It is his family and there may be issues and dynamics you aren't even aware of. You be the support he needs, behind the scenes.)

I would like you to keep in mind that mama's boys are not always the result of the mother demanding the attention of their sons and the sons complying to her every whim. Sometimes the man is so devoted to his mother that he'd do anything for her, even to the extent of unintentionally sabotaging a relationship he's in.

I knew a man who had met a young lady he really cared about. But since she lived in a different state, he wouldn't date her because he didn't want to move away from his mom. Here's the kicker — he was almost 40 years old and his mom was in great health and could take care of herself! He may have missed out on a good thing because he was cleaving to his mother.

So before you get upset with his mom for the "hold" she has on him, realize that it may not be her at all, but rather choices he makes that she's not even aware of. If this is indeed the case and his mom is unaware, it may be okay to sit down with her and express your concerns. Bringing her up to speed will allow her to be more conscious of their relationship and step back if necessary so your relationship can flourish. Be careful though — he is still her son, so be gentle in your approach and treat her feelings delicately while still being clear about how you're being affected.

WHEN HE'S INCOMMUNICADO

Are you with a guy you think is a good match except for the fact that you can't reach him and he doesn't return your calls? As a person who values communication, I can understand how this may be a source of frustration. Let's say you call your man on Monday and don't hear from him again until Wednesday or Thursday.

Living in a world where communication is at our fingertips and people are practically glued to their phones, you may find it a bit hard to believe that he hasn't had one free moment to call or text you back. It's not like you left the infamous four-word message — "We need to talk."

(If you *did* leave this message, rest assured you are being avoided. No man likes to hear those words. They automatically assume the worst and avoidance is the best way to handle it in their eyes.)

There could be a couple of reasons he didn't get back to you right away. He may have been extremely busy and knew you would want to talk for more time than he had available. This could have led him to the decision to wait and call you back when he could talk for a while.

For the considerate folks out there, you're probably thinking, "He could've at *least* sent me a text telling me that!" Right? Well, here's a news flash. Everyone is not as considerate as you are, and in a way, he felt like he was considering your feelings by not calling you and having to abruptly end the call.

Stress could be another reason he didn't call you back right away. If he was stressed about something, or irritated, he may have decided not to call because he knew he might direct his frustration toward you when it had nothing to do with you at all. Then he'd have more stress because now you're mad at him for being snappy. His solution — get a handle on a few things and then call.

I had an epiphany one day when this exact thing happened to me. I had received a phone call from someone whom I didn't mind talking to, but I was super busy that day, tired and grumpy as a result. So instead of calling right back and risk showing unwarranted irritation toward this person, I waited until later when things had settled down and I was more relaxed.

Another reason he may not have contacted you right away could be because he's not much of a talker and didn't feel like being on the phone. I know that's hard to imagine for those of us who love talking. Some guys don't prefer phone conversations and like to be brief and to the point and get off the phone.

I once knew this guy who would talk to you only once. If you called right back for something he wouldn't answer. He didn't want to be bothered again. He felt you should've gotten it out the first time you called.

In instances where you're feeling ignored or neglected, try to get to the source of what's really going on. It could be that he isn't as interested as you think and your feelings are warranted, especially if it's an ongoing issue.

However, if he goes MIA every now and then, don't fly off the handle and risk ending a relationship with someone who could really be a good fit for you.

Remember ladies, you're in the "Yellow Light" stage — don't be so quick to throw in the towel. If this guy has some potential to make it to "Green Light" status, some of these issues may be able to be worked out. As always, carefully consider, but cut the guy a little slack too.

His past

There's a saying that in order to know where you're going you have to know where you've been. I believe this applies to relationships as well. It's important to know some things about your man's past to know how your relationship may be affected.

Rebound relationships

Let's look at his relationships for a moment. Was he recently in a relationship? How much time was there between his last relationship and the one he's in with you? It's possible yours may be the rebound relationship. For those unfamiliar with the term, think in terms of basketball.

When a person goes for a layup and misses, the other players, including that person, can immediately try and take possession of the ball. No waiting is involved. The same holds true for relationships. Not much time passed between his last girlfriend and the beginning of your relationship. "Not much time" could be as little as a few weeks to a few months. It will be different for each person based on how well they deal with the breakup.

Rebound relationships can turn out to be great and everything works out fine, but most don't end up that way. In a rebound situation, most of the time he hasn't had time to fully digest the breakup. He may not have dealt with issues that eventually led to the end of the relationship.

So when he begins a new relationship with you he's bringing the old girlfriend and all of their issues with him. Relationships are hard enough on their own but the additional baggage makes it that much more difficult. He is sorting through old issues in a new relationship, and possibly taking things out on you that have to do with her. He may not even have decided to date you for who you are but because it was convenient and took his mind off of her.

Do you see how this could be unhealthy? This is not a good foundation for any relationship to be built upon.

You may wonder how this type of relationship even made it to the "Yellow Light" section, so I'll explain.

If you can identify with being in a rebound relationship, you may feel as if your guy has a lot of the qualities you'd look for but these past issues keep getting in the way. "Yellow Light" is the cautionary stage and if this describes you, it may be appropriate in your situation to exercise caution. Step back while he gets himself straightened out and maybe you two can pick up where you left off. If he hasn't dealt with his past issues, your relationship cannot flourish. You will always struggle to gain his attention, trying to find where you fit in his life.

Is this what you want for yourself?

Taking a break will give him that time to sort things through. Once he's done that, see if both of you are still interested in moving forward. If so, you stand a much better chance of success because his view of you isn't blocked by "her" and he can begin to truly see you for who you are and start to appreciate having you in his life.

Looking at his past relationships

Another thing to keep in mind is his past relationships in general. In Tyrese Gibson's book, *How to Get Out of Your Own Way,* he talks about people who are so used to drama in a relationship that if there's peace they create drama just to have a familiar environment.

Can you imagine?

If the man you're interested in is used to being in drama-filled, violent, abusive or other dysfunctional relationships, chances are he's going to seek that out in future relationships.

I remember meeting this man who described his past relationships and each one had some sort of violent episodes taking place. These were the types of relationships he seemed to attract. Until he recognizes the pattern, his next relationship will probably exhibit similar characteristics.

Also look at how long he was in previous relationships.

Did he hop from woman to woman or did his relationships have some longevity? Sometimes the brevity of the relationships may be a sign that he didn't want any serious commitment so he jumped ship and found a new partner, only to leave her in a matter of months.

On the other hand, if he was in several long-term relationships that led to breakups, this could also be a sign that he didn't want to follow through and commit to more than a boyfriend-girlfriend status.

Remember ladies, these are possibilities, not guarantees as to why he was in short- or long-term relationships. Please don't assume this applies to all men. Just use it as a guide to balance out the view you have of your guy and his relationships.

When you talk about his past relationships, who was at fault for the breakup? Does he accept any responsibility or is it all her fault, no matter which "her" he was dating at the time? A man who shows relationship and emotional maturity will not only be able to name her faults but will also be able to point out his role in the breakup. If he isn't willing to accept any responsibility for the downfall of past relationships, don't expect yours to be any different. It will always be your fault, and that's what he'll tell the next girl after you. Now, once he matures, this guy may have some potential in the "Yellow Light" zone.

I will stress this again — these topics are just things to consider before entering a relationship with someone. We tend to jump into situations headfirst and then realize it wasn't what we expected. I just want you to take a moment to read the signs so you can make a more educated decision about the man you want to date.

Still living at home? Examine why

I've talked about the past a little bit, so now let's look at his present circumstances, namely, his living situation. Suppose you met a man and everything was cool. Then you found out he was still living at home and he was over 30 years old. Before you ditch the guy and not even give him a chance, let's explore some reasons *why* he may be living at home and then decide if that's a deal breaker for you.

I have personally known at least four men over 30 who

lived at home with their parents.

Guy Number 1 (mid 30s), Jake, had been through a divorce, was out of work trying to raise two children and attend law school. In his case, coming home was not ideal for him but made the most sense in light of his circumstances. For Jake, the move back home was temporary, a means to an end while he got back on his feet. Doesn't sound quite so bad, right?

Guy Number 2 (early 30s), Emmanuel, got hurt on the job, had to quit working, which led to the loss of his house, cars, etc. He decided to go back to school for a different career. Emmanuel moved back home for the financial and emotional support in dealing with the stress of going from being on top of the world to the bottom of the barrel, from living large to starting from scratch. Do you see some potential here?

Guy Number 3 (late 30s), Andrew, was divorced, found employment, then quit his job and moved back home. He found a different, decent paying job but found it more convenient to stay at home versus move out on his own. Is your radar beeping?

Guy Number 4 (mid 30s), Nicholas, graduated from high school, considered college but never attended. He worked odd jobs for a while, moved out, moved back home, stopped working and didn't contribute to the household bills. Nicholas lived rent-free with no definitive plans to move out. Is your "Red Light" sensor flashing furiously?

These are true stories, ladies! Notice however, that each story is slightly different even though the result of the men living at home past 30 is the same. When you meet someone who falls into this category, examine the situation and then decide if his reasons for still being at home are warranted or if he's just milking his parents for what he can get.

Be careful not to make blanket statements like, "I'll never date a man who still lives at home with his mama!" Some of you might be familiar with *No Scrubs* by singing trio TLC. If he still lived at home with his mom he was definitely off their list. Take the time to evaluate each case so you don't possibly miss out on something good.

Meet his friends and family

Let's say you've met this guy, you love talking to him, you have fun together and he treats you well. The only concern is that you've been going out for a while but you've never met his friends or family. Every time you do things together it's either with your friends or just the two of you.

This scenario should be a warning. Why haven't you met his friends? Does he have any? If not, why not? Meeting and spending time around his friends gives you a more well-rounded perspective of who he is and what he's really about. If you're only around *him* all the time you only know what he tells or shows you. When you see him with his friends you get to see him "let his hair down" and get a more accurate idea of what kind of person he is.

It's possible he's more of a loner and doesn't hang out with many people. Even so, you need to be around others who know him. As I've previously mentioned, we put our best foot forward when first meeting someone. If you're able to observe and interact with him when he lets his guard down around his friends, you can see if what he's showing you is legitimate or just an act to get you interested. Of course you will want to have some alone time, but definitely make time to meet and interact with the people who are important to him. Talk to them for a different take on what he's like, how he grew up, etc.

Apply this advice to his family as well. You'd be surprised by the number of people who paint one picture of themselves and when you meet the family you see a whole different side. Watch how he interacts with his family, how often he's in touch with them and what bugs them most about one another.

I dated a man whose family didn't really care for him. The parents were more reserved with their feelings, taking more of a "we don't understand him" approach, while the siblings were more obvious with their dislike. They wouldn't invite him out when they made plans and would often make plans right in front of him. This did not change when we started dating. His few friends were either those he knew from growing up who barely stayed in touch, or ex-girlfriends. Getting to know him through his friends was difficult because they weren't around very often. The relationship didn't last, but I think if I had paid more attention to the signs his family showed, I probably wouldn't have dated him as long as I did.

All of these things will help you understand him and how he may react in certain situations. You will also get a better idea from where some of his expectations for your relationship stem. This is the stage where you're considering the potential of this relationship, so find out all you can before proceeding to the "Green Light" zone with unanswered questions.

Questions to ask yourself

You've made it to a "Yellow Light" relationship. You're comfortable with his personality, actions and background. Great! Since this is the zone where your relationship could become serious, now is the time to take some things into consideration and ask yourself some tough questions.

CAN I BE MYSELF?

First, can you truly be yourself when you're around him? Can you speak your mind without holding back for fear of how he may view you? Do you eat what you want when you're together or pick at your meal even though you're famished so he won't judge you? Conversely, do you throw healthy eating habits out the window and eat the junk he's eating so you don't appear too health conscious? Does what you wear or how you style your hair represent you or do you dress and style your hair a certain way just to impress him?

It's okay to do things your man likes — men are very visual — but if you've lost yourself in the process, you've got a problem. You should be completely at ease with your man. He should be falling in love with who you *are*, not who you've changed yourself to be. Having a man in your life should enhance you, not change you into someone *you* don't even recognize. This guy may not even stick around and he's got you in total transformation mode.

A good friend of mine puts it like this — don't change who you are to date who you like. Be yourself, no matter what! Someone out there will love you as you are and when that happens, you'll be glad you remained true to yourself.

Can I be upfront about my beliefs?

Something else to consider that is closely related to the first question is if you can be upfront about your spiritual beliefs. You also need to know if he respects or shares those beliefs.

Frequently, we enter relationships with plans to discuss spirituality later. We get so caught up in what he says, does and looks like that the fundamentals get pushed aside. If your spirituality is important to you, it should be one of the first topics you discuss, especially since it may determine if the relationship will even continue. No matter what you believe spiritually, it is important that you be clear and upfront about your beliefs and how your relationship will be impacted as a result.

Whether he respects your beliefs is vital. If you start talking about your beliefs and he dismisses them, huffs and puffs, rolls his eyes or changes the subject, you can be pretty sure he doesn't respect where you're coming from. Please don't be the kind of person who "preaches" every time you open your mouth, either, because you may get the same negative response from someone who *does* share your beliefs! You will notice conflicts throughout various areas of your relationship if he doesn't respect your beliefs.

Here are some examples: making plans on your worship

day; praying before you eat; watching certain movies; going certain places for entertainment; living together or spending the night before marriage; drinking alcohol; or having sex before marriage. The list could go on but I'm sure you get the idea.

If your spiritual beliefs are intertwined in who you are, you can't just untangle yourself, put them in a pile and place them on the shelf while dating. It doesn't work that way. Whoever you date should respect your spiritual beliefs. Better yet, he should have some of his own.

Even if he has his own spiritual beliefs, what if they differ from yours? Is one of you going to conform? Which religion will you teach your children? What if you are taught differently about how women are valued or treated? Your views regarding acceptable attire are another way your beliefs may differ. These are important areas to consider when exploring the idea of a relationship together.

Now, if the man you're with does share your beliefs, does he do more than talk about it? A lot of us call ourselves Christians, Catholics, Muslims, Buddhists, etc. because of how we were raised, but many of us fall into the "non-practicing" category. Living the life and wearing the title are two different things.

Does he attend worship services? Is he active in any ministry or just shows up when he's "supposed to"? Does he study any spiritual teachings (Qur'an, Bible, The Book of Mormon), pray and have fellowship with others who share his faith? Maybe there is a layer of dust on his materials and he struggles to bless the food when you're together. Perhaps he's new in his faith and that's fine. The question, whether he's new or very learned, is if he's living it or just talking about it.

Worshipping at the same place allows you the perfect opportunity to see for yourself if he's walking the walk. If you worship separately, visit each other's places of worship and fellowship with the members to have a better idea of where he's coming from spiritually. Study together and pray together too.

If your spiritual beliefs are foundational to who you are, he's got to be on board so your relationship can grow in the same direction and not be spiritually split down the middle.

What's my gut telling me?

Intuition is attributed to women so often that many times it's called "women's intuition." When you're dating, learn to trust your intuition. It could protect you from some bad situations and possibly even save your life.

You may be dating a man and things seem to be going well. You feel like you're moving toward the "Green Light" zone but something just doesn't feel right. You can't put your finger on it but something is off. If you are not comfortable or settled in your spirit about this relationship, examine why. Do not brush off your feelings! It could be something just under the surface in your subconscious that you can't quite pinpoint.

Be observant when you're face to face or on the phone. Does a habit he has gnaw at you? What about something he says? Perhaps one of his friendships is questionable. Maybe it seems like you're receiving information on a "need to know" basis and not getting the entire story. There are endless scenarios as to why your conscience is nudging you (he's a pedophile; he's leading a double life and already has a wife; he's cheating with another woman or man; he has abusive tendencies; he has an addiction to drugs, pornography, alcohol, gambling, etc.).

The bottom line is you are not comfortable and before the relationship progresses you need to be at peace about being with this man.

Getting to a point where you achieve this sense of peace could mean spending more time with him, his friends and family to try to pick up on details you may have previously overlooked. On the other hand, it may require you to take a step back so you can reflect on the relationship without him always there as a distraction. Sometimes a guy can tell when something's up and he'll turn up the charm a few notches so you get caught up in him again and forget what was bothering you. Be mindful of this so you are not caught off guard and end up sweeping your concerns under the rug. Let your conscience guide you. Trust your gut and follow it, even when things don't make sense.

IF HE'S OLDER, WHY IS HE INTERESTED IN SOMEONE MY AGE?

So you've met this guy. You like everything about him but you're a bit apprehensive about introducing him to your family and friends. Why? He's almost 20 years older than you and you don't know if he'll be accepted. There's a song that says age is just a number and isn't important. In some cases this is true. Let me give you a couple of perspectives to contemplate.

According to the song lyrics, age doesn't matter if you two love each other and too bad if others don't like it. I know a few people who have married men several years older and they are still together and seem to be doing well. As a matter of fact, I once dated someone almost 20 years older than I was. The age difference was not very noticeable and had nothing to do with the breakup.

It is possible that a relationship with an older man can be as successful as one with a man closer to your age. In some cases, it could be more successful since the older man may be more mature and comfortable in his skin compared to a younger man. Remember age is not an automatic sign of maturity so be wise when choosing a dating partner, regardless of his age. If dating an older man works for you, more power to you. It's fine if that's not what you prefer. You have to be in the relationship best suited to you.

On the flip side, if an older man is interested in you, make sure it's for the right reasons. From his perspective, he may like the idea of having a "pretty young thing" on his arm — proof he's still "got it like that." Also, he may want someone to take care of him as he gets older. Make sure this man is truly interested in you and not just what you can do for him.

From your perspective, you may enjoy this older man's attention for a couple of reasons. Perhaps you didn't have a strong father figure and are seeking that subconsciously from the men you date. Or maybe you want the security you feel comes with a more "seasoned" man, someone who's experienced life, is financially stable, is more settled in his life and knows what he wants out of life. Whatever reasons you have for dating an older man are fine as long as you're okay with it.

Once you're sure you're both in this relationship for the right reasons, you may still find your family is a bit resistant. This is okay. You can check in with family and friends to make sure you're not overlooking something significant. If not, continue moving forward. Even if your family and friends aren't on board, ultimately you're the one who has to be satisfied. If he's treating you well, you're happy and your relationship is healthy, hopefully they will come to accept him and his place in your life.

Does he have follow-through?

Does the man you're with have good follow-through? This question may sound familiar and it should. I talked about this in the "Red Light" section, but as with some things, this bears repeating.

When a man tells you he has plans to do something, watch for the follow-through. In a "Yellow Light" relationship this is really important because this is the time when you're deciding to hang on to or let go of the "relationship rope."

You may have noticed your man doesn't have good follow-through but brushed if off because it was little things, not things that really mattered. Be careful here. What may start as insignificant can easily spill over to more important areas.

For example, there was this guy, James. He and his girlfriend India had been together for a while. Whenever they would make plans, James would tell India he'd take care of a certain part of it, like making reservations or placing calls to someone for information. India's part would be taken care of, but days and sometimes weeks would go by before James got around to taking care of his part. Opportunities were missed, parties never happened and money was lost.

While James didn't seem too bothered, India found herself becoming less understanding of James' lackadaisical nature. She didn't want to nag because she knew that wouldn't help. At the same time, she couldn't help being frustrated by things not happening, especially after he gave his word that he would take care of them. India expressed her concern to James, who said he would make a better effort with following through. Things didn't improve at all, and actually started affecting more serious areas of their lives.

One evening they went out to eat. When James left to get the car, he discovered the car had been repossessed! He had received notices that his payments were not being received, even though he had the money directly debited from his account. James kept saying he'd call to straighten it out but never did. They were left stranded when a simple phone call could have rectified the problem and saved his credit.

For India this was the last straw. She ended the relationship shortly after. India realized that what James was showing her was all she could expect from him. This is who he was, and she wasn't going to change him. Once she came to this understanding she had to leave. His behavior was not what she wanted to endure in a long-term relationship and she didn't want to be bitter and resentful.

It's so important that the man you're planning to date has the ability to walk his talk. You do not want everything to fall on you because he's not getting it done or never be able to take him at his word because it's always just that — words. I can't stress it enough — pay attention to this area in your relationship. Lack of follow-through can affect every area of your relationship, growing like a slow-spreading disease that eventually destroys everything it touches.

Am I settling for him or comparing him to past men?

Many times after the end of a relationship we don't allow ourselves enough time to "heal and deal" — heal from past hurts and deal with the baggage we brought from the relationship. When this happens we can find ourselves settling for someone who's not a good fit or comparing the new guy to the one we left behind.

When we settle in a relationship it usually happens for a couple of reasons.

First, we've had several bad dating relationships and decide to accept whoever comes along next. Second, we haven't dated much because of high expectations and decide to lower our expectations because we're tired of waiting.

Neither reason is a good one. Dating is normally done with the intention of marrying. Why accept less than the best for yourself? Why lower your standards? You're headed toward the lifelong phase — don't lose your standards *now*. You're worth every standard you've set for yourself.

Keep the bar high, ladies!

If you settle for a man who is not compatible just to be with someone, you're setting yourself up for trouble. You will find yourself unable to engage in conversation because you don't have that much in common. You'll find yourself looking at other men with whom you have more in common, wondering why you didn't wait. You'll find yourself accepting that this is as good as it will be. You'll find yourself living with regret.

This actually happened to a friend of mine. I'll call her Renee. She had broken up with a guy with whom she thought she had a future. Heartbroken, she reconnected with someone she grew up with, William, and they began dating. Things seemed great at first, because he was a distraction from her hurting heart.

As time went on however, Renee realized it wasn't such a great match, but it wasn't that bad, so she stayed in the relationship. They married and William was elated to have such a great catch. Renee, on the other hand, found herself wondering if she had made the best decision. Coming from different educational backgrounds, William's conversation wasn't on the same level as Renee's. This was very evident when they were out with friends. William talked about work, cars and video games and would withdraw when Renee brought up politics and philosophical ideas. Plus, Renee often found herself playing "What if?" and wondering what her life might have been like had she dated or married someone else.

William and Renee are still together and Renee has come to love and accept William for who he is and the positives he brings to her life. It is just unfortunate that instead of waiting for the one truly intended for her, she settled for someone else.

The other thing we tend to do is compare the man we're with to others we've dated in the past.

Mistake! I repeat, mistake!

If you want a successful relationship you cannot compare your man to another. Remember, you are not with that other guy for a reason, probably a very good reason if you think back hard enough. So don't mess up something with promise just because your new guy doesn't do or have something your old guy did or had. Embrace your new guy for who he is and keep the past in the past.

By comparing and focusing on what you think your man is lacking, you are most likely missing out on all the great attributes he *does* have.

So what if he doesn't call you every hour just to say hello? Maybe he sends you nice flowers or shows up at your job to take you to lunch.

So what if he doesn't wine and dine you at the most exclusive restaurants? He may prepare your favorite meal from scratch or take you on a picnic for two.

So what if he doesn't buy you and your child a lot of expensive gifts? Perhaps he values quality time with you over money spent on you and would rather play or to go to the park or museum together.

So what if he's not loaded? He might make decent money, love what he does and is financially savvy with a steady stream of income.

As you enter a "Yellow Light" relationship, be mindful

that you are not settling or comparing. "Heal and deal" so you can be ready for the next guy you meet.

What do I *know* I can't live with?

"Yellow Light" relationships are where you decide if it's make or break. Does the relationship have potential or is it time to part ways?

One way to help you decide is by looking at his behavior and asking yourself, "What do I notice about him now that I *know* I can't live with?" This question is of particular importance because if there is behavior you're seeing now that you can't live with, imagine what it will be like when you're sharing the same space or worse, if you have kids and they are the same way!

Take some time to seriously consider this. For any behavior you notice that bothers you, is there a way to solve the problem? I remember meeting this guy who was very messy. I told him upfront I could not live like that and if we ever got together a maid would have to be budgeted in. So sometimes there can be a resolution and your relationship doesn't have to end.

Are things that way with the man you're dating? Can you live with what you see or is it like nails on a chalkboard every time he "does that," whatever "that" may be for you? I could give a lot of examples (chews with his mouth wide open, is always late, doesn't put things back where he got them, never wants to go out and do things, etc.) but there could be just as many pet peeves as there are people in the world. I won't bore you with a laundry list.

Have you talked to him about what bothers you? Make sure you do, because he may not even realize it's an issue for you and could be willing to work on it. He may even have a few pet peeves of his own about you! Also, be sure you're not being too critical. You will never find a perfect man because there aren't any out there. Hopefully though, you'll find the man who's perfect for you.

Maybe you have never given thought to what you know you can't live with. On the flip side, have you given any thought to what you do want in your relationships?

It would be a great help to create a personalized "negotiable — non-negotiable" chart to have handy as you date. Keep it on paper to hold yourself accountable and review it so it's familiar to you as you meet various men. Don't whip out your chart and start checking things off right in front of him — make mental notes! Appendix II gives an example of a completed chart.

As you make your chart, consider the things that matter most to you in a relationship.

Do you care if he smokes? You may be okay as long as it's outside or you may not be able to stand it at all.

What about drinking? Would you be okay with your man being a social drinker? If your relationship results in marriage, that could mean alcohol in the home. I was raised in a "dry" home (no alcohol), and I'm not willing to negotiate having alcohol in my home, for my man or even on hand for friends who stop by.

Does it matter if your man has a sense of style, or as long as he's clean and his clothes aren't wrinkled, he's alright with you?

Do you want your man to earn more than you? Must he be employed or do you mind taking care of him?

Here's one I mentioned earlier — his educational background. Must he have reached the same level of education as you in order to be considered as a potential mate?

Are you flexible on child discipline, tidiness or spending habits?

These are just a few examples of what you can include on your chart. Take some time and really evaluate yourself. Envision yourself in the future, married, with or without kids. What does that look like for you?

Pay special attention to what you *don't* see also. The things you don't see should be on your non-negotiable list — abuse, laziness, disrespect, etc. Look at the sample list in the appendix to give you an idea. Don't just copy it straight from the book either! Your chart should represent what *you* are willing or unwilling to compromise, so be specific.

Also, your lists may not be of equal length. You may find there are a few core things you must have and the rest is open to negotiation. Or, you may find you have a long list of things you aren't willing to budge on and only a few things you can be flexible about. However it looks, it is fine because the chart is designed specifically for you. Remember, this is a living, breathing document. Expect it to change along the way as you grow and mature.

Have I asked my man these questions?

Before I lead you to "Green Light," there are a few more important things to contemplate when deciding if this "Yellow Light" relationship is likely to move forward. Author and relationship expert Agness Mumbi presents four questions you should be asking the man you're involved with.

First, what are his short-term goals? Know the purpose of the relationship.

Are you just kickin' it, looking for a good time or do you want something serious? What does he want? Be clear about your intentions so no one is misunderstood or hurt down the road. You don't want to be under the assumption, or illusion, that things are becoming serious and then see him out with someone else because you two were just kickin' it and he thought you knew. You can't have an exclusive and an open relationship at the same time. One of you will be hurt. If you communicate what you want from the beginning you will have fewer problems later because you knew what you were signing up for.

The second question Agness recommends you ask is about his long-term goals.

If you have common goals it's much easier to work toward them together. Make sure you're on the same timeline in the relationship. You both may see this relationship headed toward marriage, but if you envision yourself being married in a year and a half and he's thinking five years down the road, you're going to encounter relationship strain. You'll question his feelings for you because "he still hasn't proposed!" He'll feel so much pressure and attitude from you that he may wonder if you're the right woman for him. Make sure to discuss your expectations. Don't let an unaligned timeline ruin your relationship. Be clear about what you want, hear him out and together decide how you'll proceed.

I'll combine Agness' last two points. How does your man feel about you? Notice I didn't say what he *thinks* about you. Telling you how beautiful and smart you are is a surface answer. Be careful not to allow a pat answer like that to suffice. Remember my warnings about "his smooth moves"? A man — not all men — can and will tell you want he thinks you want to hear just to keep you around. One who expresses how he feels will answer your question from the heart and delve into your character.

I remember one time I was getting to know a guy and I gave him a test, of sorts, to see how much he really knew about me. We hadn't known each other very long at all, but he was coming on strong. So, I suggested we both write down 10 things we knew about each other. I was sure he couldn't list 10 things because we never talked about anything but music and how much he liked me.

When we finished and exchanged lists, I was floored! I was right in my assumption that he didn't know many facts about me or my life, but I wasn't prepared for what he did write down. Almost everything he wrote had something to do with my character and who I was inside, not just superficial facts like where I was born or my "favorites." It was then that I realized just how interested he really was, because he was paying attention to what mattered most — my heart.

Ultimately, that's what you should notice about the man you're with. What is it about you that makes his heart sing? In a room of other beautiful women, what attracts him to you so strongly that he'd only have eyes for you? Try out the "10" list and see what you get. Talk to him too, though. And don't view this list as you looking for validation because you already know your worth. The question is, does he know your worth and what is he doing to show it?

These questions Agness suggests will give you a better idea of where the relationship stands. Ask whatever you want to know. You shouldn't ever feel intimidated about asking clear and direct questions of your man. Agness warns that it's better to ask, know and lose him now than not ask, not know and be hurt and surprised later. On that note, one thing *you* should be prepared to do is answer any questions he may ask you and be as open and honest as you'd expect him to be.

One question Agness does caution against is about marriage. She says to wait for marriage talk until your relationship is solid. Premature talk about matrimony is intimidating and could push your man away and have him thinking you're desperate. You'd be surprised how many women are in pursuit of just becoming someone's wife. If that's not how you want to come across, let the relationship progress until a more appropriate time.[1]

In a Nutshell

I have covered a lot in the "Yellow Light" section. What a journey — who knew a yellow light could be so long!

"Red Light" relationships are pretty easy to pick out — and get out of — but "Yellow Light" relationships require a bit more discernment and self-exploration. Many times a "Yellow Light" relationship is largely dependent upon you and what's okay for your life. In this section I dug a bit deeper into his personality, actions and background. This is the zone where you should be deciding to continue or end the relationship and hopefully I presented some tools for you to be better equipped when deciding. I also gave you some questions to ask yourself as well as questions to ask your man.

In a lot of cases if you're not getting what you want out of a "Yellow Light" relationship, bringing concerns to the table can be very helpful and may salvage the relationship. Communication is critical on any level, but it becomes more important as the relationship progresses. If you keep these tips in mind and make sure you've healed and are whole, you should be able to determine the direction of your relationship with relative ease.

So, ready to cruise through this yellow light? Alright then, let's pump the gas a little bit and head toward the "Green Light" zone!

Part Three

GREEN LIGHT —
CONTINUE TO PROCEED
BUT KEEP YOUR EYES OPEN!

Hopefully you didn't immediately assume your relationship is in the "Green Light" zone and skip over "Red" and "Yellow." If you did, I'm going to send you on a detour and recommend you start at the beginning and work your way through so you get the most out of this section.

For those of you who followed the signs, you made it! Welcome to the "Green Light" zone. Let's get started.

His personality

The characteristics you observe in your man's personality in a "Green Light" relationship can't even compare to previous stages. You have come to a point where his good outweighs his bad, and he's working to improve the bad. Your man has matured and is in the proper position for having a successful relationship. The following personality traits are qualities you will appreciate in your man.

HE IS HONEST AND RESPECTFUL

As you enter a "Green Light" relationship you want someone who is honest and respectful. I once read a book where the guy told his female friend that she should appreciate a lying man because his lying shows he cares and is afraid of losing her. He would rather lie to "protect" the relationship than to be honest and face the consequences.

Obviously lying is unacceptable. Your man should love and respect you enough to be honest. The relationship is very vulnerable when lying happens. Honesty is foundational to a strong, long-lasting relationship. It may be helpful to do "honesty" checks every now and then with your man just to check in and make sure you're on the same page.

Questions like "How do you feel the relationship is going — do you like the pace?" or "Where do you see us in the next six months?" or "What can I do differently to improve our relationship?" are some you might ask each other.

Dishonesty often presents itself when there's a lack of good communication because one or both of you no longer trusts the other enough to be honest. Nurture your relationship like you would a garden: consistently, purposefully and lovingly. If you do that you will create a safe and healthy environment, so when tough situations arise you both will feel comfortable enough to address the issue and continue moving forward together.

Mutual respect is also important in your relationship. This respect will show up in terms of your interests, hobbies, opinions, dreams and goals. Even when you don't agree with one another you should be able to discuss your differences while showing respect. There should not be ridiculing, criticizing or berating behavior from either of you. You are two separate individuals so naturally you are not going to agree on everything. How you handle these differences is critical to maintaining a "Green Light" relationship.

By remaining respectful with one another, you will be able to work through anything that comes up without having to sort through hurt feelings and hardened hearts to get to the real issue. Many times we mistreat the people closest to us because we expect them to always be there. Make the effort to treat each other like it's still the first date — careful with your words, considerate of the other's feelings and complimenting rather than critiquing.

He appreciates the good and bad of you

We all know there is no such thing as a perfect person. Naturally when two people enter into a relationship there will be bumps in the road. They are two different people learning to work together toward the common goal of a successful relationship.

It is important the man you're with appreciates the good and bad of who you are. Even when he thinks you are the perfect woman for him, you will still not be a perfect woman. You have flaws and you will say and do things you'll later regret. If he can appreciate you when you're screwing up as much as when things are going smoothly, you've got a keeper. This does not mean you are allowed to exploit his tolerance of your flaws by doing foolish things on purpose or without conscience.

While being tolerant of your "bad," your man should also be able to bring concerns to your attention that will help you grow out of some of your negative behaviors and more toward a better you. Trusting that he cares for you and has your best interest at heart, do your best not to meet him with resistance and attitude. Be open and objective, recognizing we all have room for growth.

He's supportive

When you have dreams and goals, there is nothing like having a support system to help you achieve them and encourage you along the way.

In a "Green Light" relationship, your guy will support you in your endeavors and should become your biggest cheerleader as you pursue your goals. I'm not only talking about lofty goals like going for a Ph.D. or starting up your own business. It could be a small goal such as honing your cooking skills or learning to speak another language.

My friend Theresa met a guy who was showing an interest in her. As they were getting to know each other, Theresa mentioned having a passion for photography and wanting to take classes to learn the craft. She tried showing him some of her recent pictures and the guy literally brushed her off and changed the subject. You can imagine how Theresa felt. It should come as no surprise that a relationship never materialized between them. This guy was already showing Theresa that he did not care about what was important to her.

At the stage where your dream or goal is just growing its roots, you don't need someone pulling it up out of the ground. You need a guy who's going to nurture and cultivate your dream right alongside of you. In a "Green Light" relationship, your guy will do exactly that. At times, he may even be more gung-ho than you are because he has that much faith in your ability, even when you get frustrated and lose focus. This is the kind of guy who is always in your corner, supports you and pushes you to dream even bigger than you imagined.

He's responsible

Responsibility is another good trait to expect in a "Green Light" relationship. "Responsible" comes in many forms:

1. He pays all of his bills and pays them on time.
2. He knows how to make and live within a budget.
3. If he is wrong he doesn't blame others but takes responsibility for his actions.
4. He maintains a decent job and is on time and productive.
5. If he makes plans he doesn't break them for no reason. If he does have to cancel, he alerts you immediately.
6. When something needs to be done he doesn't procrastinate, he gets the job done.
7. He doesn't have 10 or 11 kids by different women because he knows how to exercise self-control or, at the very least, how to protect himself.
8. Giving his word automatically implies keeping his word.

These are just a few examples of what a responsible man looks like. A man who is responsible is usually dependable as well. It is always good to know your man is someone you can count on.

He listens to you

It has been said that we have two ears and one mouth. We listen more and speak less, or at least listen twice as much as we speak. Listening is vital in any good relationship. Maybe you've heard the saying, "You hear me, but are you listening?" In relationships everywhere, even "Green Light" relationships, this is a problem.

Women have a tendency to talk for long periods of time and at inopportune times. As a result, a man hears the woman talking and sees words forming on her lips. Unfortunately, he has no idea what she's saying because he's tuned her out and turned on the autopilot responses, "uh huh," "mmm," "really?" and "yeah, I'm listening."

Here's a classic example. You know your man is into the basketball playoffs. During one of the best games of the season you decide you want to talk. About the game? No. He might actually tune in then. No, you want to talk about something completely unrelated to basketball and something that could surely wait until the game is over. To make it worse, you don't make it brief. You go on and on, through commercials and time-outs and several exciting parts of the game.

Do you really think he's listening? No, but what he is doing is getting pretty irritated and resentful and wishing he had followed his mind and watched the game somewhere else. And you get mad because he's not listening! Your behavior is rude, inconsiderate and basically tells him that what he is interested in is not as important as what you have to say. How would you feel if the shoe was on the other foot and he kept interrupting you while you were doing something you enjoyed?

Ladies, men actually do listen to women but there are some things you should know and do if you want your man to tune in:

1. Pick an appropriate time to talk, not during an activity he finds important! A good tip a friend shared is to join him during his activity and show an interest. He'll be so impressed by this that when his activity is over he'll be much more open to hearing you out.

2. Don't start with, "We need to talk." He will immediately see "Danger" signs and his "fight or flight" reflexes will kick in.

3. Think of it like boxing — get in, do a quick one-two punch and get out. Make your point, briefly, and back off.

4. Don't nag — that is a turnoff and breeds resentment and resistance. He is a grown man, not your son.

5. Leave the past behind — productive conversations cannot happen when he feels like he has never done anything right. He will shut down and tune you out.

6. Be considerate — if you want to talk, chances are this is something you've been thinking about for a while. He hasn't. Don't assume he's not listening or interested because he doesn't have immediate feedback. Once you briefly state your point or concern, give him time to think it over and express his thoughts. Be prepared for him to have a different viewpoint than you and hear him out. Otherwise, the next time he may *not* listen because he thinks you're going to do whatever you want anyway and don't really care what he thinks.

If you follow these suggestions your life will be much easier and you should notice improvements. Now please don't think the only reason men don't listen is because of the women's approach. Every man is unique, so other factors could be involved. But let's not digress. We're in the "Green Light" zone, so those other factors should have already been dealt with.

All barriers aside, a man who has made it to the "Green Light" zone will be a good listener. Not only will he hear what you say but he will actively listen to you. He will remember your concerns and address them and he will engage in conversation with you, regardless of topic — work, home, school, friends, etc. He will provide feedback and constructive criticism as needed. Your man will respect and care enough about you to know what you have to say is worth listening to.

He makes you laugh

You may find a sense of humor on your negotiable — non-negotiable chart. Many women want a man who can make them laugh. In a "Green Light" relationship your man will have a sense of humor. He will be able to laugh at himself, get you to laugh at yourself and be able to enjoy the lighter side of life. This doesn't mean he is immature. There is a difference between childlike and childish behavior.

Childlike means he has the ability to see things from an innocent point of view or just be silly every once in a while. Maybe he picks some dandelions and gives them to you because he thought about how you like the color yellow. Perhaps he pulls you outside when it's sprinkling to play in the rain.

Childish behavior usually includes selfishness and irrational tendencies. For example, if you have to get off the phone to take care of something, he gets upset because you can't talk longer. Or he will only play games with you that he has a good chance of winning. If he does play a game he's not good at, he won't put forth any effort.

A man who has a sense of humor will help you maintain balance in your life and not take everything so seriously. In your relationship, laughter can be healing. The Bible says a merry heart works like medicine.[1] Laughter is even good for tightening your ab muscles!

So what are you waiting for? Live, love and lighten up in your relationship and appreciate your man's sense of humor.

He's patient and understanding

Look for a man who is patient when in a "Green Light" relationship. One of the fruits of the Spirit in the Bible is patience[2] and having that attribute is so beneficial. A patient man gives you the freedom to be yourself.

If you mess up, you know he's not going to blow up at you. When you don't understand something, he doesn't get irritated and criticize you. He stops, explains and explains again if necessary.

When you forget something, he doesn't berate you for having to repeat himself. He just tells you again and helps you come up with a way to remember it next time.

During an "open mouth, insert foot" moment, he won't lash out and use his words against you, but will help diffuse the situation and probably even give you a chance to redeem yourself.

The patience your man shows you can be a good indicator of the patience he will show with your children. Keep in mind that no man is perfect so he may get grouchy every once in a while. However, at the core of his being is a big reservoir of patience and that is what counts.

A man who is patient will be understanding as well. The singing group Xscape sings about wanting understanding from their men. This is definitely a "Green Light" trait to have. A man who understands, or "gets you," is like icing on the cake in a relationship.

An understanding man is one who knows you inside and out and knows how to relate to you. He doesn't get easily ruffled about things others may not be able to handle because he knows how you are. He is more patient because he has spent time learning what makes you tick from listening and observing. A man who is understanding is more empathetic when you are dealing with "stuff" and knows when to comfort and when to give you space.

He understands you to the point that he can finish your sentences and can probably tell you some things about yourself you haven't even realized yet.

He's compassionate

Another trait you will find in your "Green Light" relationship is compassion.

Jesus was the best example of this. He demonstrated compassion with everyone he encountered no matter what. Down to his last breath, he showed concern for others.

A man who shows compassion is one who is in touch with his emotions. He is still a "manly man," but he has a heart for people. If he sees a need, he will try to help. Some others may be quick to judge or dismiss a person in need. Not your man.

He will lend a hand without seeking a reward. Your guy will be the one helping someone load their groceries in their car while he's got ice cream waiting in his. He will be the one to assist in changing a flat tire, even when he has someplace else to be. Your guy will sign up as a Big Brother to try and keep another boy engaged, even while he's raising his own son.

This compassionate nature will be instilled in the lives of his children as well. The kids will grow up showing compassion because it is such a natural part of who their dad is, and is all they know to do. Having a man with a good heart is such a blessing. Not only will his kind and caring nature be shown to you, so many others' lives will be touched as well, with a legacy that will live on long after he's gone.

He's trustworthy

If you survey people and ask what the most important thing is in a relationship, the majority will tell you it's trust. Without trust the whole relationship has little chance of survival. In a "Green Light" relationship, your man will be someone you can trust and someone who trusts you. Knowing you can trust your man will give you a sense of confidence you may never have experienced before.

Most think of trust in terms of affairs, but trust can also be more basic than that.

When you're with a man you can trust, you can share your fears and insecurities and know they won't be used against you. Trust lets you confide in your man and know whatever you tell him will stay with him. An established trust between you and your guy lets you try new and uncomfortable things without worry of being teased or ridiculed. Trust allows you to be vulnerable.

In relation to affairs, trust is essential. In the "Green Light" zone you will have a man you can trust. If he says he'll be a certain place you won't ever have a reason to doubt that. He may even have female friends. To establish trust in this area, he will introduce you to each of them and hang out all together from time to time. If he and a female friend maintain phone contact, you will not be paranoid because you know he can be trusted.

Your trust should be so established that your man will be comfortable coming to you and mentioning being approached by another woman because he knows you won't flip out over it. When you trust your man you won't become a detective, checking through his phone and pockets or practically stalking him. You will know he is committed to you because he gave his word and has given you no reason not to believe him.

Your man will show his trust in you in the same ways.

He may call, email or text you throughout the day because he's thinking about you, not because he's suspicious. Your male friends won't cause him to be jealous because he will get to know them. When their names come up in conversation he won't get upset because he knows you only want to be with him. He will feel comfortable opening up with you and possibly sharing things he never told anyone else because he trusts you will handle the information delicately.

When it comes to trust there are usually two extremes — trusting too much, usually too early in the relationship, and not trusting enough, usually due to baggage.

In your "Green Light" relationship, it is important to

find the proper balance. As your relationship progresses, so will your level of trust. Allow yourselves to really open up with one another and experience a level of intimacy like never before.

His actions

In a "Red Light" relationship, a man's actions will literally push you away. A "Yellow Light" relationship will cause you to question his motives and sincerity. When you're in a "Green Light" relationship you will notice a difference in your man's actions. You will find yourself being drawn to this type of man. The following actions are sure signs your man is on his way to becoming husband material.

YOU ARE FRIENDS FIRST

One example is how he gets to know you. While he may be very attracted to you, he takes the time to get to know you — get this, ladies — with no expectations of a reward. That's right, this man spends his time with you, talking, doing things together. He is able to invest a considerable amount of time without looking for a return on investment. He doesn't pressure you for sex but enjoys your company and allows the gift of your time to be his reward. This is the type of guy who can walk you to your door and be okay with a hug and a kiss on the cheek. He won't be mad that he wasn't invited in "to talk," because we know there would be little talking going on!

He is the man who gets to know the things that matter to you and doesn't allow sex to distract him from knowing the real you. Let me clarify quickly — this doesn't mean he won't think about sex or that he won't slip up and try something (he *is* human). It means he'll exercise some willpower to control himself and respect that your body is to be treasured by your husband.

Essentially, you will be "courted" by your man. Courting is an old fashioned term, but for those dating with the intention of marriage, courting is actually quite appropriate. In his book, *I Kissed Dating Goodbye*, Joshua Harris tells his story of becoming serious about finding the life partner God picked for him.

He no longer dated for kicks, but took his time, sought Godly counsel and courted his girlfriend, now wife, Shannon. But it started with him being willing to get to know her without the expectation of a reward, just pure and simple friendship. He outlines the necessary steps in this process in his book.[1]

Without friendship as the foundation the relationship is being built on shaky ground. That is not a good place to be when you're vowing "'til death do us part."

He lives his life for God

When you find yourself in a "Green Light" relationship you want a man who is secure in his relationship with God. I acknowledge there are other religions and beliefs but God is who I am familiar with so I will write about Him.

As I mentioned in the "Yellow Light" section, he should have his own relationship with God and not be hanging onto the coattails of his parents or you. He must know God for himself so if he were all alone he'd still have a solid foundation.

Knowing God, your man will also know his role as a Godly man, husband and father. This will be extremely important if your relationship becomes more serious and you begin to discuss marriage.

In understanding his role, he should have some Godly men in his close circle of friends. Guys talk, just as women do and it is vital your man receive counsel from men who love the Lord. This allows him to be accountable to other men with shared beliefs. They won't feed him advice that's popular but will hold him to a standard and make sure he's living up to his Godly potential. These men may be the very ones reminding him what a gem he has in you and be quite influential in the forward progression of your relationship. As your relationship grows you will come to greatly appreciate the role these friends have in his life.

Even outside of his friends, a man with a relationship with God will understand how valuable you are and will treat you accordingly. You may find yourself craving a level of intimacy he won't allow because he respects you too much to go there.

A friend of mine, Brian, made a decision not to kiss another woman on the lips until he married her. In this day and age, that's just about unheard of. Brian knew himself well enough to know the temptations that came along with kissing so he removed the possibility of slipping by setting boundaries. That was a clear indicator of his love for God and his respect for who he dated. He didn't want either of them to end up living with regret down the road.

Brian is actually engaged to be married as this book is being written. That shows it is possible to have boundaries and a good relationship at the same time.

Lastly, a man with a relationship with God should be concerned with your spiritual growth as well. Maybe the two of you study the Bible or worship together and discuss the message afterward. As a future husband and father, your man should be preparing himself to function in those roles. Part of that includes making sure his life partner is spiritually connected as well.

He takes his time, but not too much time

I mentioned earlier that we tend to get so caught up in the outward characteristics of a person that we miss out on what he or she is really about. Often this is to our detriment. As you head toward a "Green Light" relationship, your man will take his time and get to know you.

Your outward appearance is most likely what initially attracted him. Your inner beauty and character are what will capture his heart. As he gets to know you he may get to a point where he's looking for a more serious relationship. However, he will still exercise caution and he will not rush as he pursues you.

When you're considering a long-term investment of any kind, the last thing you do is act in haste. The same is true of relationships. You take the necessary time to think it through, pray about it and seek guidance before making a commitment. This is the example he will follow. The intended goal is a long-lasting relationship and by moving too quickly he runs the risk of being involved in a relationship not suited for him. He could possibly destroy a relationship that actually had potential for success.

The key is for him to take his time, but not take too much time and possibly lose you to someone else. Herein lies the delicate balance. If he's trusting God and not acting in fear, he will know if you are the one. He won't waste any time letting you know and he will begin to confidently pursue you.

Learn to appreciate a man who takes his time. This trait will probably surface throughout your relationship. When important decisions need to be made you will find your man's ability to step back and evaluate a situation to be invaluable.

He's ready to head a household

A "Green Light" relationship could often lead to marriage so it makes sense to ensure your man is ready to head a household. Being the head of a household does not mean your man becomes king of the castle and you bow down to him. There should be give and take but he should be the one who guides the family down the right path. He may have to make some of the tough decisions that affect the family — buckling down on spending, taking a second job, etc.

Your man will remember that running a household efficiently requires a team effort in every area. He will include you in the decision-making process. His role is like that of a team leader on your job. Sometimes he may have to make executive decisions, but any decisions made will be in the best interest of the family.

Your man will also be ready to set the example for the family to follow. He will be quick to apologize and be emotionally available. Sharing tasks around the home and respecting each member of the household are other things your man will do. Understand that "household" can mean just the two of you or it can include children.

If your household includes children the relationship dynamics change. You should be in agreement as to how you raise them, discipline them, how many children you actually want and if adoption is an option.

As head of the household, your man will be prepared to discipline the children — not just be their playmate. He will also understand the need for grace at times to allow the children to learn and grow. If either or both of you are bringing children into the relationship you definitely want to make sure there is no favoritism or resentment toward the stepchild by either of you or other siblings. You set the standard and allow your actions to be the example for the other children to follow. Blended families can sometimes be a tough transition, but as you are in your "Green Light" relationship, use this time to figure out how you're going to make it work.

He's in it for the Long Haul: Children with Special Needs

Another thing to weigh is children born with special needs. Are you both open to raising a child with a disability? This could mean your child will always require care, even after becoming "of age." It may also mean additional household expenses including adaptive equipment, therapy sessions or frequent doctor and hospital visits.

You will not always know if your child will have a disability before delivery. Sometimes you are just blessed with a child who needs a bit more care and who manages to steal your heart in the process. At times, the disability appears as the child gets older (deafness, blindness, etc.), or as the result of a disease or trauma.

Of the families spoken to or read about, none of them wished their child was never born or wished they were born without a disability. Their reason? Life wouldn't be as complete without that child and without the disability the child wouldn't be the same one they had grown to love.

There are some tests you can take to see if either or both of you carry traits for certain diseases such as sickle cell anemia, cystic fibrosis, Tay-sachs, Huntington's disease or various neurological disorders. The results of a test like this may or may not affect your decision to have children together, but you will at least be informed.

Some of the diseases I mentioned can be very agonizing to live with and you may decide not to risk putting your child through lifelong pain. Maybe you choose to adopt instead. On the other hand, you may consider any child God gives you a blessing, not bother with the test at all and trust that God will only give you what you can handle.

Ultimately the choice is yours, but it's a choice you must discuss and make together. Some marriages don't survive after a child with special needs is born because the possibility was never discussed beforehand. I would encourage you to remove as many barriers ahead of time so your "Green Light" relationship can continue to flourish, even when challenges present themselves along the way.

HE PUTS HIS FAMILY FIRST

Along the same lines, as your "Green Light" relationship progresses, your man will be prepared to put his family first. That doesn't mean he won't have to work late occasionally or that he won't spend time with his friends. What it means is his family will be the first priority and everything else will fall in line after that. We often forget what matters most because so many other things demand our attention immediately.

As the future provider for your family, your man could easily get stuck in the mindset of doing whatever it takes to ensure his family is taken care of financially to the point that it negatively impacts the family. This mindset-affected behavior could lead to increased overtime, which means less family time. Maybe you have to place some boundaries on work — weekends off-limits; or no work on Sunday; or home by dinner time each night; or no bringing work to bed; or schedule around school sports and activities.

Time spent together as a family is just as, if not more, important as *money* spent on a family. Make sure you discuss what is involved in living within your means so no one has to work like crazy, and remember "taking care" of one's family is not just about money. All aspects should be nurtured — the physical, emotional, intellectual and spiritual. Compliment your man on the financial stability he offers and how he provides for the family by being present. His presence alone can make such a huge difference for the entire family's success.

With regard to his friends and hanging out, there has to be a balance. While you're dating, of course he'll spend time with you and time with his friends. If the two of you end up married, his days of bachelorhood will officially end. In order for your marriage and family to thrive, there must be time invested.

That can't happen if he is — this applies to you also — constantly hanging out with friends. He will definitely need bonding time with them but the single outings won't outweigh the family time. Maybe instead of hanging out *all* day Saturday with the guys, he cuts it down to two or three hours. There can be times when you go on group dates to maintain friendships and once the children come, family outings will happen too.

The bottom line here is balance. If you're in a "Green Light" relationship, your guy should already have this in mind and you should definitely talk about it before moving forward.

He believes in monogamy

This next trait should go without saying, but to be clear, I'll say it anyway and keep it moving. In a "Green Light" relationship, monogamy is a given. Your man is a one-woman man, at all times. He knows that anything less than his best in this area immediately removes him from his "Green Light" status and places him at serious risk of losing you.

Monogamy includes physical and emotional relationships with other women. Your man is aware of his temptations and steers clear of them. He shares his feelings with you, and tells you if there have been tempting situations and the two of you work together to resolve any concerns.

The only way for your relationship to remain in the "Green Light" zone is for you both to be upfront and honest in all things, comfortable or uncomfortable. The ability to do this helps establish a trust relationship and builds a level of intimacy you will need for a lasting union.

He is a man with a plan

In a "Green Light" relationship it is so important your man has a plan for his life.

What is his vision? Does he have his life mapped out for the next five, 10, 20, 50 years? If he is going to be the head of a household he needs to have some goals he's working toward. A man cannot lead if he has no direction. Without a vision of where he sees himself, he will be aimless and not reach any goals he may have set.

Here's an example of a plan your man may have: "Over the next two years I plan to eliminate any debt I may have so when I get married I will not bring debt into the relationship. I would like to be married and starting a family within five years. In about a year or year and a half after we're married, I expect my wife to have the choice of working outside the home or not holding a job. If we don't already own a home when we marry, we will be able to buy one within three years. I plan to branch out and start my own business in 10 years and hire employees just after the first year.

"I will maintain my desired weight of 180 lbs. by working out regularly and cooking healthy food at home more than eating out. I plan to be socially active by continuing the activities I'm currently involved in and adding others of interest without becoming stressed by being too busy. I plan to travel somewhere once a year and try something new at least twice a year.

"I will continue to be actively involved in my church and grow spiritually by studying my Bible at least three times a week, attending worship services and Bible study weekly and praying throughout the day. I will meet with my accountability partner twice a month or more to ensure I'm living a life of integrity.

"When I retire at age 55, I plan to live off of my investments. I will choose three organizations to donate to and will volunteer at least once a week. My wife and I will have the financial stability to pay for what we want in cash and enjoy life and retirement completely debt free."

This is just one example of the kind of vision your man may have for himself and his family. A man without goals will never accomplish anything. As long as he has set goals, he will succeed, even if those goals change. Why? He will still be working toward something so he will continue to move forward.

You definitely want to be on board with a man who has a plan. Together the two of you will go far — the possibilities are endless.

He has a financial plan

I talked about a man with a plan, or vision, for his life. Having a financial plan is a large part of that. Since you're in a "Green Light" relationship, you're preparing yourself for marriage. You are probably aware that one of the top reasons people divorce is due to money issues — either not having enough or disagreements on how it is spent.

Take the time now to develop your own financial plan and make sure your man has one of his own. Talk about what your financial future will look like and be thorough.

A man who has made it to the "Green Light" zone does not have a large amount of debt, if any. This man has a good credit history, pays his bills on time and does not live above what he can afford. He has a budget set for himself.

If he has some debt, he should have a plan for becoming debt free and be working toward that. Knowing it is not good to bring debt into a marriage, he will be doing all he can to eliminate his debt prior to asking anyone's hand in marriage.

Your man should be able to show you and explain his financial plan. He will be financially independent and working toward wealth building and financial success.

Dave Ramsey is a well-known Christian financial guru who has helped thousands of people achieve financial success. He teaches common sense principles and believes in living debt-free and helping others once financially able.

For those who don't know how to do this on their own, he has a class called Financial Peace University (FPU). In it, you learn the steps he recommends to gain financial freedom. Each step is explained in detail and broken down into manageable parts. I highly recommend this course before moving toward marriage. That way you're of one mind financially, which greatly increases your chances for a successful marriage.

Remember, marriage is for mature, responsible people and that most certainly includes being financially responsible.

In a Nutshell

By this point in your journey the ride should be a lot smoother. You are more comfortable in who you are and are either embarking or preparing to embark upon a journey with a man who is compatible with you and has a lot of potential as a future life partner.

In this "Green Light" section you learned the attributes of a man who's worth consideration for a long-term relationship. I emphasized the importance of a man with a plan, financial and in other areas, as well as the value of having a man who is your friend first. I also touched on the need for him to understand his role as a Godly man, father and husband. In order for him to be any good as the spiritual leader he must know how to carry out the duties required of each role.

As you continue to proceed while keeping your eyes open I hope you use your "negotiable — non-negotiable" chart you made in Part Two to help you recognize when the next man in your life is worth the long-term investment.

Conclusion

The purpose of the book was to help you recognize common traps some men set while dating. I also wanted to provide you with the necessary tools to avoid harmful relationships by analyzing his actions, exploring his background and observing his personality.

If you find yourself in a "Red Light" relationship, get out now! Remember, the guy you're with should enhance the happiness, joy, peace and love you already have within. If he's not doing that, or you notice some of the traits I mentioned in Part One, it's time to walk away from that unhealthy situation and prepare yourself for someone better suited to you.

Learn how to let go of your baggage, "heal and deal" and validate yourself. There is great value in knowing yourself and being comfortable and confident in who you are.

"Yellow Light" relationships can be a bit more challenging to discern. Communication is critical in this zone, as it will most likely determine the direction of the relationship. Take the time to honestly evaluate your relationship with your man. Make sure it lines up with what you want for yourself. This is not the time to settle — this is your life and you shouldn't be accepting anything less than what's best for you.

Keep in mind what's best for you may not look like others' idea of what's best for you. Know yourself well enough to not be swayed by others' opinions. Still keep an open mind. Sometimes people offer valid "outside perspective" advice. Ultimately, though, the choice is yours.

Go ahead and make that chart to document the things you are and are not willing to negotiate when it comes to dating. It is a lot easier to recognize what you don't want when you already have an idea of what you do desire in a man.

The goal is for everyone to be involved in a "Green Light" relationship. It may be a long journey of learning for some and a quicker trip for others. Either way, you'll get there, and when you do, you'll realize the journey was completely worth it. Getting to the point where you are healthy and whole is fantastic. Being involved with someone who "gets you" and enhances you, even better!

As you stopped off in the "Red Light" zone, journeyed through the "Yellow Light" zone and finally cruised on into the "Green Light" zone, I hope you have been inspired, enlightened and empowered to become your best self and be open to receiving all God has for you.

Lastly, remember, marriage is for mature, responsible people.

You *knew* I had to say it one more time!

Appendix I

Background Check web sites

www.intelius.com/

http://www.backgroundcheck.org/

http://www.backgroundchecks.com/

http://www.snoopstation.com/

http://www.ussearch.com/consumer/background-check/

Appendix II

Negotiable — Non-negotiable chart

Negotiable	Non-negotiable
Shy v. outgoing	Job (with benefits)
Education level	Non-smoking
Social drinking	Takes responsibility
Fashion sense	(house, work, finances,
Cooking ability	children, marriage)
Writing ability	Honest
(grammar, spelling)	Trustworthy
Tidiness	Self-motivated
Physique	Respectful (of himself, of me)
Foul language	Relationship with God
Already has children	Not abusive (physical, emotional,
Divorced or widowed	mental)
Attractiveness	No pornography
Punctuality	Good hygiene habits
Homebody v. socialite	Unselfish
Organized	Supportive
Likes to travel	Dependable
Has his own transportation	Has balance (work, family, play)
	Financially responsible
	(invests wisely, no major debt,
	good credit history/score)
	Common interests
	Not possessive
	Generous (with time and money)
	Considerate (of me, my time)
	Takes care of body/overall health
	Follows through
	Willing to apologize when wrong
	Positive attitude
	Open communication
	Common discipline habits
	Hard-working

Recommended Reading List

I Kissed Dating Goodbye, Joshua Harris

Act Like A Lady, Think Like A Man: What Men Really Think about Love, Relationships, Intimacy and Commitment, Steve Harvey

Woman, Thou Art Loosed!: Healing the Wounds of the Past, T. D. Jakes

He's Just Not That Into You: The No Excuses Truth to Understanding Guys, Greg Behrendt and Liz Tuccillo

The 5 Love Languages: The Secret to Love That Lasts, Gary Chapman

How to Get Out of Your Own Way, Tyrese Gibson

The Total Money Makeover: A Proven Plan for Financial Fitness, Dave Ramsey

In the Meantime: Finding Yourself and The Love You Want, Iyanla Vanzant

Endnotes

Part One: Red Light

Chapter Two

[1] Planned Parenthood. (2012). *Withdrawal (Pull Out Method)*. Retrieved July 3, 2012 from http://www.plannedparenthood.org/health-topics/birth-control/withdrawal-pull-out-method-4218.htm

Chapter Three

[1] Our Pathway Home. (n.d.). *'Dry Drunk' Family Patterns*. Retrieved July 3, 2012 from http://cyquest.com/pathway/patterns_addiction.html

[2] Basic Background Check, available from http://www.peoplesmart.com/PSP.aspx?_act=searchids-mkt1&cam=1981&gclid=CNr3-d_UwrICFahaMgod_H8AGg. Retrieved August 7, 2012

[3] Minimum Prices for Background Checks, available from http://www.backgroundcheck.org/. Retrieved August 7, 2012

[4] Maximum Prices for Background Checks, available from http://www.ussearch.com/consumer/background-check/. Retrieved August 7, 2012

[5] Basic Background Check Information. Retrieved August 7, 2012 from
http://www.ussearch.com/consumer/background-check/

Part Two: Yellow Light

Chapter Seven
[1] Mumbi, A. (2009, August 25). 4 Important Questions You Should Ask Your Boyfriend. *EzineArticles.* Retrieved October 25, 2009, from http://EzineArticles.com/2816294

Part Three: Green Light

Chapter Eight
[1] Proverbs 17:22, King James Version

[2] Galatians 5:22, Amplified Bible

Chapter Nine
[1] Harris, J. (1996). *I Kissed Dating Goodbye.* Sisters, Oregon: Multnomah Books. pp. 205-221.

Index

A

abstinence until marriage standard, 20–23, 53–54, 107–108
abusive behavior
    in bad boys, 8–9
    in his parents, 33
    isolating you from friends and family, 12–13
    in past relationships, 65
    trust issues and, 7
actions (his), 49–61, 105–117
    being friends first, 105–106
    children with special needs and, 110–112
    heading a household, 109–110
    lack of availability, 59–61
    life plans, 114–117
    living for God, 106–108
    male and female roles, 54–56, 109–110
    monogamy beliefs, 25–28, 101–102, 113–114
    mother-son relationships, 56–59
    pressuring you for sex, 21–23, 53–54
    putting family first, 112–113
    real interest in you, 49–51
    saying "I love you" too soon, 51–53
    taking his time, 108–109
    words not matching, 43–44
affairs, 25–28, 101–102, 113–114
affection, physical. *See* sexual intimacy
age differences, 75–77

B

background checks, 34–36, 123
background of dates, as red light concern, 31–36
bad boys, 7–10
being yourself, 71–72
Bible references, 57, 99
birth control, 23–24
blended families, 110
breakups, accepting responsibility for, 66

C

childlike vs. childish behavior, 98
children
    birth control for prevention of, 23–24
    deciding to have, 29–30, 111
    discipline of, 110
    number of children/children's mothers, 14–15
    with special needs, 110–112
communication
    about differing sex standards, 10–12, 21–23, 53–54
    about marriage timelines, 85, 87
    about pet peeves, 83
    about real interest in you, 51
    about selfishness, 47
    about yellow light concerns, 89, 121
    compromise and, 47–48
    "I" statements in, 48
    incommunicado men, 59–61
    lack of respect, addressing, 42
    listening to what he's telling you, 17–18, 28–30
    listening to you, 95–98
    mother-son relationship boundaries and, 58–59
    patience and understanding in, 99–100
    questions for him, 84–87
    smooth talkers, 42–43, 86
    tips for successful, 96–97
    when actions don't match words, 43–44
compassion, 100–101
compromise, 47–48
contraception, 23–24
courtship, 106
credit-worthiness, as yellow light concern, 46

D

disabilities, children with, 110–112
discussing problems. *See* communication
dishonesty. *See* lies
disposition, as red light concern, 3–4
divorce, of married men, 28

F

family
    isolating you from, 12–13
    meeting his, 13, 31–33, 68–69
    mother-son relationships, 33, 56–59
    older men concerns, 75–77
    putting family first, 112–113
    See also children; parents
financial issues. *See* money issues
Financial Peace University (FPU), 116–117
first impressions, 29, 30, 46
follow-through
    as red light concern, 18
    as yellow light concern, 43–44, 77–79
friends
    being friends first, 105–106
    influence of, in spiritual matters, 107
    isolating you from, 12–13
    meeting his, 13, 31–33, 68–69
    older men concerns, 77
    putting family first, 112–113

G

genetic testing, 111
Gibson, Tyrese, 65
gifts, potential dangers of, 9
goals
    life plans, 114–117
    in the relationship, 85
    supportiveness in, 93–94
green light relationships
    compassion in, 100–101
    defined, 90
    honesty and respect in, 91–92
    listening to you in, 95–98
    patience and understanding in, 99–100, 108–109
    responsibility in, 94–95
    sense of humor in, 98–99
    summary of, 119, 122
    supportiveness in, 93–94
    trustworthiness in, 101–103
gut feelings, trusting, 74–75

H

Harris, Joshua, 106
heading a household, 109–110
healing from and dealing with the past, 79–82
He's Just Not That Into You (movie), 44
honesty, 43, 91–92
    See also lies
housework roles, 54–56
How to Get Out of Your Own Way (Gibson), 65

I

I Kissed Dating Goodbye (Harris), 106
"I love you," saying too soon, 51–53
"I" statements, 48
incommunicado men, 59–61
infidelity, 25–28, 101–102, 113–114
insecurities
    as red light concern, 4–5
    as yellow light concern, 52–53
interest, showing, 44, 49–51
intimacy, physical. *See* sexual intimacy
isolating you from friends and family, as red light concern, 12–13

L

lies
    about STI testing, 24–25
    background checks to verify truth, 34–36, 123
    by married/committed men, 26–27
    by smooth talkers, 42–43
    unacceptability of, 91–92
life plans, 114–117
lines often used, 18–23
listening

to what he's telling you, 17–18, 28–30
to you, 95–98
See also communication
living for God, 106–108
living situations
  alleged "roommate" arrangements, 14–15, 26
  living at home, 66–68
long-term goals (his), 85, 114–115

M

make or break issues, 82–84
  See also negotiable–non-negotiable charts
male and female roles, 54–56, 109–110
mama's boys, 57–59
marriage
  abstinence standard, 20–23, 53–54, 107–108
  clarifying timeline for, 10–11, 85, 87
  courtship prior to, 106
  heading a household and, 109–110
  maturity and responsibility needed for, 10, 23, 117, 122
  monogamy importance, 25–28, 101–102, 113–114
  mother-son relationships and, 57–58
  putting family first, 112–113
married/committed men, as red light concern, 25–28
maturity and responsibility
  age and, 76
  in birth control use, 23–24
  breakups and, 66
  in green light relationships, 94–95
  with money issues, 45–47, 51–52, 116–117
  needed for marriage, 10, 23, 117, 122
  number of children/children's mothers and, 14–15
meeting family/friends, 13, 31–33, 68–69
mixed signals. *See* communication

money issues
  financial plans, 116–117
  male and female roles, 55–56
  paying bills for him, 51–52
  as yellow light concern, 45–47
monogamy, importance of, 25–28, 101–102, 113–114
mother-son relationships, 33, 56–59
moving too soon, too fast
  as red light concern, 10–12
  as yellow light concern, 51–53
Mumbi, Agness, 85–87

N

negotiable–non-negotiable charts, 83–84, 119, 122, 125
nice guys vs. bad boys, 7–10
number of children/children's mothers, 14–15

O

older men, 75–77

P

parents
  interaction with and between his, 33
  living at home, 66–68
  meeting his, 13, 31–33
  mother-son relationships, 33, 56–59
patience and understanding, 99–100, 108–109
personality (his), 3–15, 91–103
  actions not matching words, 43–44
  compassion, 100–101
  disposition, 3–4
  honesty and respect, 91–92
  insecurities, 4–5
  isolating you from friends and family, 12–13
  lack of respect, 41–42
  listening to you, 95–98
  money personality, 45–47
  moving too soon, too fast, 10–12, 51–53
  number of children/children's

mothers, 14–15
patience and understanding, 99–100, 108–109
selfishness, 47–48
sense of humor, 98–99
smooth talkers, 42–43
supportiveness, 93–94
trustworthiness, 6–7, 101–103
See also maturity and responsibility
pet peeves, 82–84
planning skills, 114–117
previous relationships
comparing him to, 79, 81–82
rebound relationships and, 63–64
as yellow light concern, 65–66

Q

questions for him, 84–87
questions to ask yourself, 71–87
age differences, 75–77
being myself, 71–72
comparing him to others, 79, 81–82
follow-through capability, 77–79
gut feelings, 74–75
make or break issues, 82–84
questions for him, 84–87
settling, 79–81
sharing spiritual beliefs, 72–74

R

Ramsey, Dave, 116–117
rebound relationships, 63–64
red light relationships
background of dates, 31–36
bad boys, 7–10
birth control reluctance, 23–24
defined, 2
disposition and, 3–4
insecurities and, 4–5
isolating you from friends and family, 12–13
lines often used, 18–23
listening to what he's telling you, 17–18, 28–30
married/committed men, 25–28
moving too soon, too fast, 10–12

number of children/children's mothers, 14–15, 26
sexually transmitted infections and, 24–25
summary of, 37–39, 121
telling you what you want to hear, 17–18, 25–28
trust issues, 6–7
relationships. *See* green light relationships; marriage; previous relationships; red light relationships; yellow light relationships
respect
in green light relationships, 91–92
for parents, 33, 56
for sex standards, 20–21, 23, 107–108
for spiritual beliefs, 72–73
as yellow light concern, 41–42
responsibility. *See* maturity and responsibility

S

self-improvement, importance of, 37–38
selfishness, 47–48
sense of humor, 98–99
settling, 79–81
sexual intimacy
abstinence until marriage standard, 20–23, 53–54, 107–108
vs. being friends first, 105–106
birth control, 23–24
differing interpretations of, 11–12
lines often used, 18–23
moving too soon, too fast, 10–12, 51–52
pressuring you for sex, 21–23, 53–54
sexually transmitted infections (STIs), 24–25
short-term goals (his), 85
smooth moves, 17–30
birth control reluctance, 23–24
lines often used, 18–23
listening to what he's telling you, 17–18, 28–30

by married/committed men, 25–28
sexually transmitted infections and, 24–25
smooth talkers, 42–43
telling you what you want to hear, 17–18, 86
smooth talkers, 42–43
special needs children, 110–112
spirituality
living for God, 106–108
sharing beliefs about, 72–74
stepchildren, 110
stress, communication and, 60
supportiveness, in green light relationships, 93–94

T

taking time, in relationships, 108–109
telling you what you want to hear
married/committed men, 25–28
as red light concern, 17–18
as yellow light concern, 42–43, 86
10 things list, 86–87
trust issues
background checks, 34–36, 123
in green light relationships, 101–103, 114
gut feelings, 74–75
as red light concern, 6–7

V

values
abstinence until marriage standard, 20–23, 53–54, 107–108
sharing spiritual beliefs, 72–74

W

"We need to talk" messages, 59–60, 96
women's intuition, 74–75

X

Xscape (singing group), 99

Y

yellow light relationships
actions not matching words, 43–44
defined, 40
lack of availability and, 59–61
lack of respect and, 41–42
living at home and, 66–68
male and female roles, 54–56
meeting family/friends, 68–69
money personality, 45–47
mother-son relationships, 56–59
past relationships, 65–66
pressuring you for sex, 53–54
real interest in you, 49–51
rebound relationships, 63–64
saying "I love you" too soon, 51–53
selfishness and, 47–48
smooth talkers, 42–43
summary of, 89, 121–122

Booking and Order Form

To order copies of *Warning Signs:
What every woman should know — A dating guide*

By mail:
Ambergris Press
P.O. Box 7364
Flint MI 48507-0364

By internet:
www.ambergrispress.com
www.warningsignsbook.com

By bookstore:
Ask your favorite bookstore to order *Warning Signs: What every woman should know — A dating guide* (ISBN 9780988624696)

Become a Facebook fan of *Warning Signs: What every woman should know — A dating guide:*
www.facebook.com/WarningSignsBook

To book the author for speaking engagements or workshops:
danielleeward@gmail.com
www.danielleward.me

Find Danielle:
On LinkedIn: www.linkedin.com/in/danielleeward
On Facebook: https://www.facebook.com/author.danielle.e.ward